Cambridge Elements ☰

Elements in Digital Literary Studies
edited by
Katherine Bode
Australian National University
Adam Hammond
University of Toronto
Gabriel Hankins
Clemson University

THE SHAPES OF STORIES

Sentiment Analysis for Narrative

Katherine Elkins
Kenyon College

CAMBRIDGE
UNIVERSITY PRESS

CAMBRIDGE
UNIVERSITY PRESS

University Printing House, Cambridge CB2 8BS, United Kingdom

One Liberty Plaza, 20th Floor, New York, NY 10006, USA

477 Williamstown Road, Port Melbourne, VIC 3207, Australia

314–321, 3rd Floor, Plot 3, Splendor Forum, Jasola District Centre,
New Delhi – 110025, India

103 Penang Road, #05–06/07, Visioncrest Commercial, Singapore 238467

Cambridge University Press is part of the University of Cambridge.

It furthers the University's mission by disseminating knowledge in the pursuit of
education, learning, and research at the highest international levels of excellence.

www.cambridge.org
Information on this title: www.cambridge.org/9781009270397
DOI: 10.1017/9781009270403

© Katherine Elkins 2022

First published 2022

A catalogue record for this publication is available from the British Library.

ISBN 978-1-009-27039-7 Paperback
ISSN 2633-4399 (online)
ISSN 2633-4380 (print)

The Shapes of Stories

Sentiment Analysis for Narrative

Elements in Digital Literary Studies

DOI: 10.1017/9781009270403
First published online: July 2022

Katherine Elkins
Kenyon College

Author for correspondence: Katherine Elkins, elkinsk@kenyon.edu

Abstract: Sentiment analysis has gained widespread adoption in many fields but not – until now – in literary studies. Scholars have lacked a robust methodology that adapts the tool to the skills and questions central to literary scholars. Also lacking has been quantitative data to help the scholar choose between the many models. Which model is best for which narrative and why? By comparing more than three dozen models, including the latest deep learning artificial intelligence (AI), the author details how to choose the correct model – or set of models – depending on the unique affective fingerprint of a narrative. The author also demonstrates how to combine a clustered close reading of textual cruxes in order to interpret a narrative. By analyzing a diverse and cross-cultural range of texts in a series of case studies, the Element highlights new insights into the many shapes of stories.

Keywords: sentiment analysis, narrative studies, digital humanities, affective AI, emotional arc

ISBNs: 9781009270397 (PB), 9781009270403 (OC)
ISSNs: 2633-4399 (online), 2633-4380 (print)

Contents

1 The Birth of a Field

In 2016 Adrienne LaFrance, writing for *The Atlantic*, described "The Six Main Types of Storytelling, As Identified by an AI." A few months later the *Washington Post* announced that "Researchers Have Quantified What Makes Us Love Harry Potter." A group led by Andrew J. Reagan had published research suggesting that "The Emotional Arc of Stories Is Dominated by Six Basic Shapes," along with an example from the Harry Potter series as shown in Figure 1.

These findings offered proof for Kurt Vonnegut's thesis that all stories have simple shapes. Vonnegut wrote a master's thesis in anthropology for the University of Chicago on these simple shapes of stories. It was rejected but he later reprised it in a lecture that is now available on YouTube. He shows us shapes that look like curved waves that undulate above and below a horizontal axis. The horizontal x-axis plots the unfolding time of the story and the y-axis maps the rise and fall of misery and good fortune. As just one example, Vonnegut draws the shape of the Cinderella fairy tale. As shown in Figure 2, the story starts with misery since Cinderella can't go to the ball like her stepsisters. Then the shape climbs with Cinderella's good fortune since the fairy godmother helps her to go after all. The arc falls again with Cinderella's departure from the ball at midnight before rising one last time with the happy ending when Cinderella is reunited with her prince.

Anthropology as a field has long explored the shapes of stories, whether the folktales of Vladimir Propp and Claude Levi-Strauss – on which more in a moment – or the fairy tales invoked by Vonnegut. Apparently even anthropologists have their limits, however; Vonnegut's thesis was rejected. In the video Vonnegut gives a deadpan performance as we hear the audience chuckle. The simple shape of the story is both fun and, when he points it out, all too simple. Too fun and too simple is Vonnegut's own surmise of why it was rejected, as he writes in *Palm Sunday*.

Vonnegut muses in his talk that there's no reason why the "beautiful shapes" of stories can't be fed into a computer. He was right, although today we are more likely to see these beautiful shapes emerge as output rather than input. Early work modeling the emotional arc of *Romeo and Juliet* was first undertaken by David Bamman, who hired human labelers on Mechanical Turk to analyze the play scene by scene. Ted Underwood then compared their findings with a computational analysis and published the results on his blog, *The Stone and the Shell*. The computational graph that Underwood created, shown in Figure 3, relied on a recent tool developed by Matthew Jockers: Syuzhet. Underwood found that his model and Bamman's comported quite well.

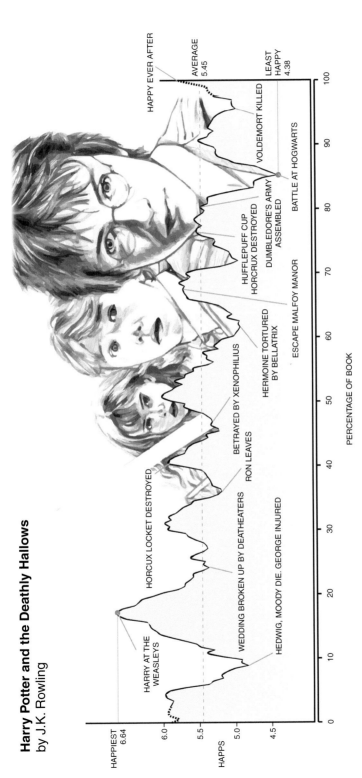

Figure 1 Sentiment analysis of Rowling's *Harry Potter and the Deathly Hallows* (Reagan, 2016)

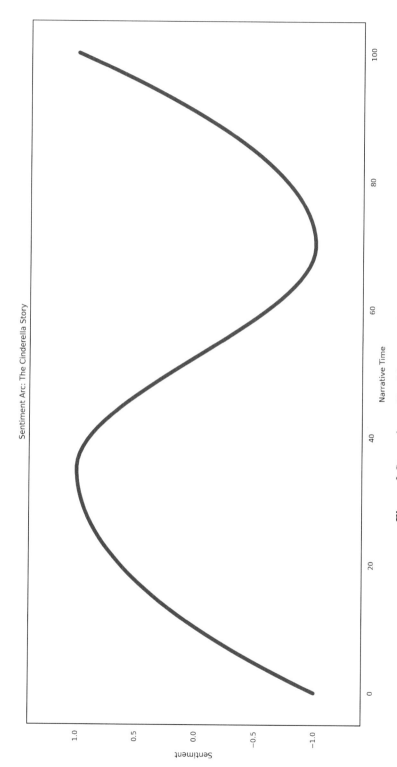

Figure 2 Story shape: Double person in the hole

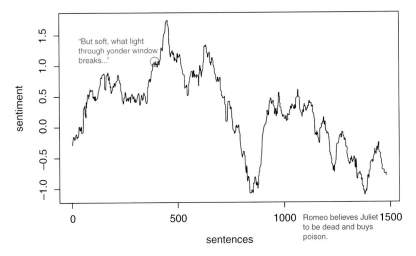

Figure 3 Sentiment analysis of Shakespeare's *Romeo and Juliet* (Underwood, 2015)

Jockers, who had developed the tool, was also comparing it against hand-coded novels. He too found that the results comport fairly well with human judgment in James Joyce's *Portrait of the Artist As a Young Man* (2015). Tragedy proved easy to graph, but it's a bit more surprising that *Portrait of the Artist As a Young Man* evinced such a clear emotional arc. *Portrait* combines elements of life writing alongside representations of consciousness, aesthetic theory, and even church sermons – hardly a story of the kind Vonnegut describes.

The year after these developments hit the mainstream press Jon Chun and I decided to try out another modernist novel. Would a novel known for being relatively plotless – Virginia Woolf's *To the Lighthouse* – still evince an underlying structure? We found the answer to be yes. This finding suggests that the typical periodization of the modernist novel as highly experimental in form may require more nuance since we have found that modernist novels can in fact surface classic story shapes.

Underwood poses another periodization question. *Romeo and Juliet* may be quite easy to graph, he suggests, given that tragedy conforms to a typical structure. But what about the realist novel, which the literary historian Ian Watt describes as moving away from plots that are so predictable? Could realist novels be harder to plot than many modernist novels *or* tragedy? In fact, we have found in our lab that this approach can reveal latent structure in a wide variety of narrative genres well beyond the realist novel, from screenplays to *Shark Tank* episodes, political speeches to poems, judicial opinions to financial news reporting.

These findings make evident the fact that this method for surfacing arcs does not expose plot directly. Instead, it surfaces an underlying sentiment structure that occurs even when very little happens plot-wise. Reagan and his group call it an emotional arc and, if you try out their Story Lab tool, the "Hedonometer," you can explore the emotional arc within a no-code web browser environment. Their tool offers keywords that contribute to the valence of the sliding window of text. Yet, looking at the list of words and the emotional arc, it's hard to make sense of it from a scholarly point of view. What is happening in each section? How well does it comport with a critic's understanding of the narrative? It is impossible to tell, although one can certainly guess if one knows the novel well.

Jockers's work moves toward an approach more familiar to literary scholars by assessing how well the points of inflection – the peaks and valleys of the sentiment arc – comport with the passages often selected for close reading. In the case of his own investigations, he finds peak detection of the minima and maxima comport surprisingly well to the key passages or "cruxes" often chosen by scholars. Our exploration of more than one hundred novels confirms that the tool often – though not always – surfaces what many scholars might consider key crux points.

Within the digital humanities, sentiment analysis once necessitated the use of the specialized statistical programming language R. Only recently have many of us been working to make it available to those who work in the much more popular general programming language Python. Jon Chun has also worked to make available a much wider array of tools and approaches using easily accessible low-code Jupyter notebooks.[1] SentimentArcs offers a wide range of sentiment models from simpler to the more complex. We have spent several years exploring these many models, many narratives, and many ways of "smoothing" the arc to produce the shapes that Reagan and his group describe. Section 2 on methods and the case studies that follow in Section 3 rely on the foundational SentimentArcs corpus that we created.[2]

---

[1] Infinite thanks are due to Jon Chun, without whom this Element could not have been written.

[2] Chun explains:

> SentimentArcs' corpora consists of 25 narratives selected to create a diverse set of well recognized novels that can serve as a benchmark for future studies. The composition of the corpora was limited by the effect of copyright laws as well as historical imbalances. Most works were obtained from US and Australian Gutenberg Projects (Gutenberg, 2021) (Project Gutenberg, 2021a) . . . Several dimensions of diversity were considered for inclusion including popularity, period, genre, topic, style and author diversity. The first version of our corpus includes only English, although Proust and Homer are included in translation. SentimentArcs has processed a larger set of novels, including some in foreign languages. The initial reference corpus is in English since performance across all ensemble models was uneven in less resourced languages (Dashtipour et al.,

What we have found is that narrative sentiment arc is much more complicated than the Hedonometer might lead one to believe. For one thing, there are many different tools with different methods of surfacing sentiment, and sometimes the thirty-five different models we've worked with can seem like thirty-five different "readers" in the room. We are far from having a single model that is empirically "best" for all narratives and sometimes even the state-of-the-art models can struggle with specific texts. Different tools, we have found, work better for different texts, and the model and text must be jointly optimized for best results. Finding the best fit between a model and a particular narrative can be challenging. What follows in these pages is the description of an ensemble method that relies on considering a variety of models to arrive at an optimal fit.

Narratives are "fuzzy," and in computational terms we need to think of probabilistic confidence intervals rather than simple deterministic point values. There is no way to derive a model that gives simple black-and-white answers with 100 percent certainty. We are also assuredly not in the realm of the hypothesis-driven scientific method that aims to test if our data reveal underlying phenomena distinct from random chance by using tests of statistical significance. Nor, unfortunately, can we use what is termed supervised learning, which relies on a labeled data set to train models that can evaluate new unseen data sets. We cannot label the emotional arc of Virginia Woolf's *To the Lighthouse* and expect it to accurately model Joseph Conrad's *Heart of Darkness*, for example. Each narrative is unique in its own way, and there is no universal ground truth we can use to compare, evaluate, and select the "best" sentiment model.

Instead we are in the realm of probabilistic models and what is termed exploratory data analysis. Optimal model fit will depend on the unique linguistic nature of each narrative, and determination of that fit relies on what is called a human-in-the-loop (Yeruva et al., 2020) to evaluate that fit and arbitrate between the differing results of competing models. A human-in-the-loop or, in the case of narrative analysis, a critic-in-the-loop, presupposes that all models are wrong and that the ultimate judgment as to which model is useful can be determined only by a human reader. This approach stresses the importance of the human expert and relies on computational models as an aid rather than the final arbiter of any ground truth. For that reason, what follows will describe a method that can be used to

---

2016). SentimentArcs' corpora spans approximately 2300 years from Homer's *Odyssey* to the 2019 *Machines like Me* by award-winning author, Ian McEwan ... In sum, the corpora includes (1) the two most popular novels on Gutenberg.org (Project Gutenberg, 2021b), (2) eight of the fifteen most assigned novels at top US universities (EAB, 2021), and (3) three works that have sold over 20 million copies (Books, 2021). There are eight works by women, two by African-Americans and five works by two LGBTQ authors. Britain leads with 15 authors followed by 6 Americans and one each from France, Russia, North Africa and Ancient Greece.

assist the reader but never replace the reader. Chun's SentimentArcs makes it easier for scholars to quickly visualize all of this nuance for any narrative, and his tool offers efficient methods to quickly assess divergences that still need to be evaluated by the critic. The pace of innovation in the field is rapid and tools will continue to evolve and change. Nonetheless, methods for evaluation of the models will remain the same and we already have enough tools that work well to begin leveraging them to yield insights in the field.

Until now, there have been a few key reasons sentiment analysis has not been widely adopted. First, it has been difficult to determine the optimal model beyond comparing a few models on specific texts and engaging in guesswork. Second, there has been an absence of clear methodology to get the most out of the approach. Watching both professional scholars and students in the classroom struggle with how to evaluate and validate models has convinced us that best practices – firmly grounded in an understanding of the approach – are needed. Finally, scholars have until now failed to demonstrate how sentiment analysis can yield insights into narrative that are compelling for most scholars. As a scholar who has published widely using more traditional methods, my goal here is to leverage this new approach to yield interpretative results in ways that align with more traditional approaches.

In the following pages I start with the history of the shapes of stories and of sentiment analysis for narrative before turning to the ways in which this approach dovetails with recent trends in literary scholarship. Then I detail methodological aspects of using the tool: close reading of cruxes for the validation of a single arc, evaluation of an ensemble of models for best fit, and assessment of questions surrounding what is called "smoothing." Finally I turn to interpreting the models as a method of yielding insights into individual novels as well as surfacing larger questions surrounding narrative more generally. From an investigation of plotless and postmodern novels to life writing, explorations of race, gender, and colonialism to issues of translation, sentiment analysis can assist the reader in surfacing interpretive insights. Moreover, it has much to show us about the role of emotion in narrative, as well as both the singularity and the shared structure of narratives – the shape and the shapes – of stories.

Even with such a useful approach, the real work begins where the model ends. In spite of the headline, sentiment analysis doesn't actually offer quantitative reasons for why we love Harry Potter, nor does it confirm that all stories share the same shape, though many do once smoothed. For all the newness of the approach, the traditional methods of the literary critic are still needed: intimate knowledge of the narrative and a close reading of the language of sentiment that forms the peaks and valleys of the arc. The scholarly questions raised by the approach are thus more complex than we first expected, and in a good way. For now the aim of what follows is to suggest the many different ways and contexts in which sentiment analysis can be leveraged to explore new questions that may be of interest to literary scholars. Because much of what we analyze in literature are "edge cases" – because so much canonical literature strays from predictable use of language – sentiment analysis is often stretched, sometimes to its limit, by the challenge narratives present.

It is therefore not surprising that sentiment analysis has been widely adopted in other fields before it has been in narrative studies. Mäntylä, Graziotin, and Kuutila (2018) summarize the evolution of the approach, first to mine customer opinion and, more recently, to explore social media. Meanwhile the number of papers published in the field continues to grow exponentially. Our hope is that literary studies will finally adopt it as one approach – among many – to explore the shapes of stories.

1.1 A Brief History

Do stories have shapes? Aristotle, in *Poetics*, was the first to suggest that they do. In tragedy, he wrote, all events are interconnected and demonstrate the change in the protagonist's fortune. The shape is determined by these events, which give rise to the protagonist's happiness and misery. Plot and the protagonist's emotions are thus tightly interwoven, and together they form the shape of tragedy. Aristotle was also the first to suggest the importance of emotion in the experience of tragedy. Spectators experience a *catharsis* when they are able to react to the tragedy with feelings of pity and fear. The shape of the story lies in the events that trace the happiness and misery of the protagonist, but this shape of tragedy is intimately connected to our own emotional reaction.

In the nineteenth century novelist and playwright Gustav Freytag outlined a pyramid-like structure for a dramatic plot in which he described a rising and falling structure of actions that forms a triangular shape. In the mid-twentieth century the literary critic Northrop Frye, building on Freytag's pyramid, suggested a U and an inverted U structure depending on whether it was a comedy (U) or a tragedy (inverted U).

In addition to these simple shapes, others have tried to determine the underlying shapes of stories by breaking stories into atomic units. Vladimir Propp focused on the linear unfolding of events, classifying each action as a discrete unit and demonstrating that, in Russian folktales, these essential actions always occur in the same order. Claude Levi-Strauss also broke stories into atomic units, called mythemes, that can be explained, he suggested, by thought processes common to all cultures. Both the formalism of Propp and the structuralism of Levi-Strauss, then, were attempts to determine the underlying shape of stories through an analysis of its most essential elements, whether plot or theme.

Levi-Strauss was probably influenced by the work of Carl Jung, whose theories of unconscious thought formed the basis for an explanation for basic archetypes. Instead of plot events or themes, a Jungian approach focuses on the most basic elements of a "hero" or protagonist, thereby defining archetypes, the most discrete elements of a character, as they are found across stories. Building on these many ways of suggesting that all stories are crafted from the same elements, Joseph Campbell popularized the notion of a "monomyth" and the "hero's journey," combining fundamental plot elements with character archetypes to suggest similar patterns in all stories. More recently, Christopher Booker categorized stories in his *Seven Basic Plots*. He employs the same kind of elemental breakdown of action, giving examples of seven basic plots that include "Overcoming the Monster" and "The Quest."

In addition to all these simple shapes, atomic events, and character types as shown in the timeline of Figure 4, there are recent applications to film. George Lucas credits Campbell's work with helping him bring his *Star Wars* draft to completion, and the final version relies on the fundamentals laid down in the hero's journey. Dan Harmon has further popularized this approach by emphasizing the "story circle" underlying many well-known movies. Indeed this story circle is a common method used in creative writing workshops and classes today. If you are wondering whether screenplays evince the same underlying shape found in novels, our preliminary investigations suggest they often do.

These shapes of stories look a bit different from the triangles and U's described by the first theorists in the field. One question remains, however. You may be wondering, "Are all stories as simple as Cinderella?" and you would have good reason. As the highly esteemed narratologist Jim Phelan once asked me, "If all stories have the same basic shapes, why should we care?" A very good question indeed.

1.2 Aren't All Stories Unique?

Shapes fed into (or spewed out of) computers don't interest most literary scholars, and this may be one reason that modeling the simple shapes of stories has failed to gain traction in the field. With our attention to the particular

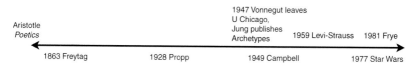

Figure 4 Theories of story shape

passage and a concern with the unique nature of each story, simple shapes may even seem to work against our attempt to explore the individual aspects of each story. A good way to think about this is to imagine oneself standing at a certain distance from the story. From a distance, one can see the simple shapes that all stories share. From a closer perspective, each story has a pattern as unique as a fingerprint.

While I will touch on questions of the simple shapes of stories, therefore, the primary focus of what follows will be on exploring the unique fingerprint of stories, the *many shapes* of stories rather than the *simple shape* of all stories. In the following sections I'll show how sentiment arcs can help us understand particular texts as well as the differences between the works of a single author. Moreover, as more of us employ these approaches and, collectively, we graph a larger number of stories, we should be able to explore even more deeply the ways in which stories differ from each other. Collectively, we can begin to create a new body of research that investigates differences in sentiment arcs across time periods and genres, across different cultures, and for different readers.

Exploring sentiment arcs, perhaps much like the experience of narrative, can be quite emotional: thrilling and puzzling, inspiring and confusing. Those inclined to think of computational approaches as binary and definitive – all zeros and ones – will be surprised to find that the process of analyzing a sentiment arc feels very much like what we already do. It offers an exploratory method at its very best, often inspiring more questions than answers and requiring close reading and analytical skills to yield insight.

The risk of all computational approaches, of course, is that some will view the computer's output and assume the computer has done the work for them. In fact, knowing what to do with the graph is not obvious at all, and it's taken hundreds of novels and several years of exploration to develop a reliable method. Those who haven't read the story may not be able to glean much beyond the simple shape. Those who understand the story but don't understand the approach will similarly be at a loss. One has to understand how the model works in order to make sense of what it shows.

For that reason this Element will spend quite a bit of time moving between describing the approach and giving examples of how to leverage this understanding by incorporating literary methods. The focus here will be on the kinds of questions that literary scholars already ask using more traditional methods. All too often work in digital humanities is too technical to be of interest to many literary scholars. Oftentimes digital humanists also ask questions that are more in line with the fields of data analytics or the broad sweep of literary history than with what many of us do in examining the unique aspects of a particular story.

A middle reading, rather than a distant reading, marries close analysis of language with the larger, middle view of the narrative shape before stepping back for that much more distant perspective of only a very few simple shapes. But, first, let's begin with the research that has focused on stories from that more distant perspective of their very simple shapes.

1.3 Sentiment Analysis for Narrative

Some of the earliest work using sentiment analysis (2008–2012) on long-form texts focused on religious ones like the Quran, the Book of Mormon, and the Bible. Likely inspired by this work, Matthew Jockers first blogged about it in June 2014 and created his tool called Syuzhet. Subsequent blogs and a chapter in his book *Macroanalysis* followed. In 2015 Annie Swafford critiqued aspects of the Syuzhet package and a very lively and productive discussion followed.

Swafford noted that the simple shapes produced by Jockers's initial smoothing algorithm created "ringing effects" at the beginning and end of the sentiment graphs. In other words, there was distortion at the boundary points of the model due to the fast Fourier transform (FFT) smoothing algorithm, which assumes the first and last sentiment values should be neutral or zero valued. In narrative terms this means that Syuzhet could get the beginning and endings of the narrative very wrong. This ringing effect is a well-known property of the FFT method Jockers used to normalize the lengths of different sentiment series (i.e. to normalize the differing lengths of stories) and smooth it to create the simple shape of the curves. There are various ways to address this, but ultimately Jockers decided to replace the FFT with a method called the discrete cosine transform (DCT). The DCT, unlike the FFT, does not assume boundary conditions that give rise to beginning and ending "ringing effects." A second, more serious critique was leveled by Swafford, however – that Syuzhet was unable to factor in negation and intensification and thus made fundamental errors in misclassifying sentiment. For the field of digital humanities, this very public critique of Syuzhet had a definite chilling effect even as sentiment analysis as a method was gaining widespread adoption elsewhere.

Nonetheless some entered the fray. In 2016 a group of mathematicians and statisticians led by Andrew Reagan at the University of Vermont's Story Lab produced research using a different smoothing method to analyze a large corpus of stories from Project Gutenberg. Using Gutenberg.org's corpus of fiction, Reagan's group analyzed 1,327 texts and found that when "smoothed" to reduce random variation and to emphasize the overall trend, stories fell roughly into six basic shapes:

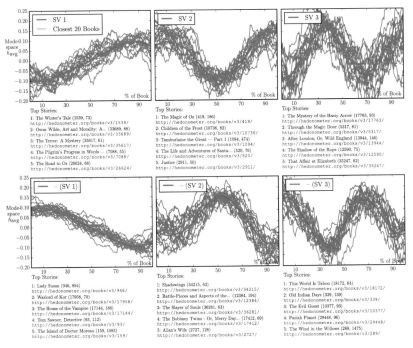

Figure 5 Six basic shapes of stories (Reagan, 2016)

- "Rags to riches" (rise).
- "Tragedy," or "Riches to rags" (fall).
- "Man in a hole" (fall-rise).
- "Icarus" (rise-fall).
- "Cinderella" (rise-fall-rise).
- "Oedipus" (fall-rise-fall).[3]

Reagan's group lists the most common stories associated with each, as can be seen in Figure 5. The researchers include plays, not just narrative fiction, and indeed one of the clearest instances of the tragedy arc is (not surprisingly) Shakespeare's *Romeo and Juliet*. On the other hand, some of Shakespeare's plays that we typically categorize as tragedies do not exhibit a typical tragic shape. While Jockers worked on the level of a single novel, these researchers employed the more common method of distant reading. Still their approach was not without problems. Ben Schmidt rightly noted that their corpus was not well filtered to include fiction only, and Chun has

---

[3] Reagan's group employed a smoothing method from linear algebra, singular value decomposition (SVD), followed by hierarchical clustering using self-organizing maps (SOM).

not been able to replicate the findings using a sampling of models and methods available with SentimentArcs.

While Underwood theorizes tragedies might be easier to graph, their linguistic sparsity – that is, the absence of much of the language of novels that communicates sentiment through the representation of consciousness, gesture, and facial expression – may present other challenges. Sentiment can be conveyed in a myriad of ways in theater, for example with lighting, staging, voice, and gesture. In the case of film and television artificial intelligence (AI) researchers are developing multimodal methods that take into account sound (e.g. voice pitch and speaking rate), image (e.g. facial expression and body pose), and even video (e.g. gesture and body movement).[4] Still we have found that the language of screenplays yields promising results: in the case of a Harry Potter film adaptation, for example, the novel and the screenplay surface similar arcs.

Here I focus on narratives that do not rely on non-textual information. In spite of the flaws, Reagan and his group inspired our work, not only because they felt the method still had much to offer to help us understand stories but also because their work actually raised interesting questions for literary scholars. Surprisingly, Freytag's pyramid – the rise and fall of the "Icarus" story – is very poorly represented among the stories sampled on Gutenberg. Yet, in terms of download frequency, this shape is one of the most popular. While rare, in other words, the triangular shape is quite well-liked.

Better classification of genres – plays, novels, nonfiction – might also offer further insights as to whether this dramatic pyramid structure is more common in a corpus of plays than in novels, for example, or more popular (judged by download frequency) in one genre than the other. One of the other interesting findings from Reagan's group is that some stories fall outside these six shapes. They chose to focus on the six predominant ones, they explain, because most variance can be classified within one of the six basic shapes, with fewer texts falling into more complex wave shapes. From a statistical point of view, this makes sense since they smoothed their stories to achieve this result.

Perhaps the most common technique to smooth noisy time series is the sliding window method, specifically, the simple moving average (SMA) or rolling mean method. Given a time series (e.g. a sequence of values like sentence sentiment scores over the course of a novel), a fixed-sized window slides over a percentage of the entire text's corpus, stepping forward one

---

[4] See www.mckinsey.com/industries/technology-media-and-telecommunications/our-insights/ai-in-storytelling# for a description of visual and audio analysis of the film *Up*.

sentence at a time. The sentiment of the center sentence is assigned a value based upon a measure of statistical centrality.[5] This technique smooths out sudden short peaks and valleys, thereby revealing a smoother long-term trend.[6]

Reagan's group was more concerned with the average story, rather than any outliers, and various methods of smoothing like the sliding window can help surface these "average" shapes. The group also focused on the six basic shapes in order to align their research with the work by Christopher Booker on the seven basic shapes of stories. It is important to stress, however, that *most* stories may share one of six basic shapes under this paradigm of smoothing the granular shape to abstract out a pattern of a few curves. Some that don't are more complex shapes with multiple curves. While Reagan et al. don't find many of their stories conforming to these other, curvier shapes, they find that the double person-in-a-hole shape, shown in Figure 6, is actually quite popular in its download frequency.

Like the Icarus shape, it is relatively rare, yet seemingly quite popular. More work is needed to gain a better understanding of all these nuances. How might we better measure popularity? Is the Gutenberg corpus truly representative? Both popularity, as imperfectly measured through frequency of downloads, and prevalence, as measured in such a limited corpus, deserve further investigation.

Matthew Jockers, along with coauthor Jodie Archers, makes a different but provocative claim in *The Bestseller Code*. Bestsellers often have these more complex, up-and-down, "heartbeat" patterns that resemble this double wave that is both rare and popular according to Reagan's lab. While we believe that more research is needed to confirm and likely qualify this bestseller claim, Reagan's group does offer additional data to suggest that this more complex pattern is popular. One possible avenue of research in coming years will be to investigate not only how common these "heartbeat" curves are among more popular books but also whether there has been any change in the composition of "bestsellers" (however one determines such a list) over time. The limitations of the Gutenberg corpus, composed of stories that are no longer under copyright, does not allow us to ask this question, and we would need to assemble a better corpus in order to answer it, however provisionally. Alternatively, our own

---

5 The most common sliding window, which is used by SentimentArcs, employs the arithmetic mean. The window assigns equal weights to all values within the window in order to compute the center sentiment value. Other sliding windows give the center value the greatest weight while decaying weights as they approach both ends of the window.

6 Jockers's DCT, Reagan's SVD, and SentimentArcs' SMA are all common smoothing techniques, although SMA is the most common and easily interpretable. Both Chun's SentimentArcs and Jockers's Syuzhet also use LOWESS smoothing, discussed further on.

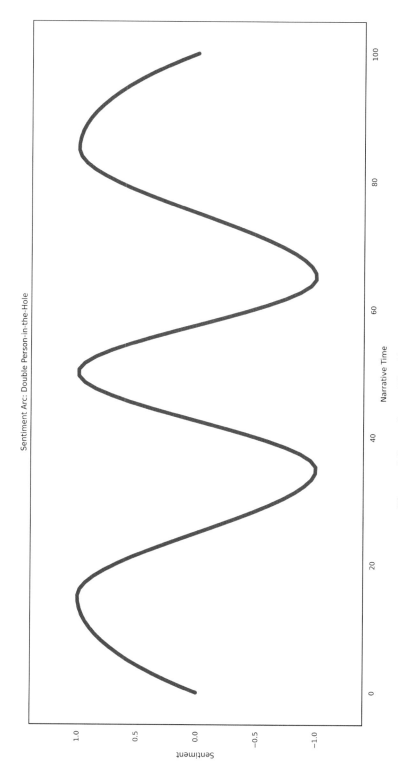

Figure 6 Story shape: The Cinderella story

research suggests, as does the research of Reagan's group, that these types of curves may be found widely across time periods and genres.

Jon Chun and I first began working with Syuzhet in 2017. The ringing issue didn't concern us very much because Jockers had replaced FFT, but also because it's simply the case that this kind of statistical model does poorly when it lacks enough data to extract a clear signal – at the beginning of the narrative, before there is much text to analyze, and at the very end, when the model again runs out of data. As George Box famously says, "All models are wrong, but some models are useful." In this case there is no doubt that sentiment analysis is not as useful for mapping beginnings and endings, though there are methods for addressing this limitation that I will discuss later. Those in fields that routinely use models are more likely to assume a certain degree of "wrong-ness" while also imagining that the model could be useful.

Since that time, and based on extensive research, however, we have become skeptical about applying common smoothing methods like the ones used by Jockers and Reagan's group.[7] Some smoothing methods presuppose an under-lying shape, which they then surface. For this reason the analysis in subsequent pages relies on a much simpler simple moving average (SMA) that affords a more granular and precise shape with fewer assumptions.

Annie Swafford's more powerful critique of naive lexical approaches to sentiment analysis concerned us more at the beginning. How problematic was the failure to take into account negation and intensification? As one example, a simple lexical tool might inaccurately value the sentence "I don't hate you" as a negative emotion based on the word "hate" while failing to take into account the negation with the use of the word "don't." This is potentially a much more serious problem, one that we sought to interrogate carefully in our first work with Syuzhet published on arXiv in 2019.

Was the failure to account for negation and intensification and the ensuing misclassification a serious problem? We compared Syuzhet with a tool, VADER, that does account for intensification and negation. We found that these types of sentiment errors were equally distributed around the average sentiment scores such that they statistically canceled each other out. In other words, both VADER and Syuzhet largely agreed on overall sentiment plots. Swafford's critiques were not insurmountable. Moreover, it would not be too difficult to incorporate the best of both Syuzhet and VADER – the benefits of a very large lexicon and the usefulness of tracking negation and intensification.

---

[7] Smoothing methods imported from other domains like electrical engineering often assume a strong underlying structure in the frequency domain, whether FFT or DCT. Jonathan Scott Enderle comes to the same conclusion about SVD. See his detailed discussion at https://senderle .github.io/svd-noise.

In fact, Tyler Rinker explored combining the Syuzhet lexicon with the heuristics of VADER and suggested that this model performed well on the edge cases that Annie Swafford identified as problems for Syuzhet. We have found that Rinker's approach often still tracks fairly closely to Syuzhet, but it performs slightly better in certain cases and we use it quite often in our lab.

New techniques for smoothing (Gao et al., 2016), as well as adaptive filtering and multifractal analysis (Hu et al., 2019) are pushing the field in new directions. Many are also using simple machine learning (ML) models that are popular in industry to serve as familiar baselines for academic research. Common ML sentiment classifier models, however, require more engineering decisions.[8] We include a popular ML model, TextBlob, in the pages that follow.

Meanwhile, more work has been done in distant reading using this technique. Morin and Acerbi (2017), for example, argue for the "birth of the cool" with a decline of emotional language in Anglophone fiction over the past two centuries. Kim, Padó, and Klinger (2017) have tried large-scale classification of genre by sentiment arc. Some have even used sentiment analysis to track the literary reputation of authors (Taboada, Gillies, and McFetridge 2006). Do speeches have a narrative arc? Tanveer, Samren, Baten, and Hoque (2018) have found TED Talks exhibit sentiment arcs as well. Boyd, Blackburn, and Pennebaker (2020) suggest that nonfiction narratives like these exhibit distinct shapes, and we continue to explore these areas of research in our lab.

Still one of the elements missing until now is a way to adapt the approach for more traditional methods of literary analysis. We favor working with the representation of the shape of the story that gives us the more unique fingerprint and not those more general shapes favored by Reagan and others. Moreover, even this more unique sentiment arc should always be evaluated for whether it comports with the gold standard of expert human analysis, and one can do this by employing what we call a middle reading of the peaks and valleys that is proximal rather than exact.

While our initial research called for close reading of peaks, our subsequent work has convinced us that a better method is clustered close reading. This is because, as you'll see, the various ways of graphing the arc generally comport, but the slight variations offered by different tools and distinct lexicons create just enough of a variation in crux point positions that it's important to consider these points indicative of an area of the text – often slightly larger than a single

---

[8] Popular models include decision trees, support vector machines (SVMs), and naive Bayes. More decisions must be made, such as how exactly the text is vectorized and which sentiment corpus to use to train models (e.g. movie/IMDB, restaurant/Yelp or product/Amazon reviews). The SentimentArcs ensemble includes a family of these good old-fashioned artificial intelligences (GOFAIs) should you wish to explore.

passage – rather than the single sentence or paragraph favored by close reading. A better term for the overall approach is thus "middle reading," since the passage sizes are often slightly larger than those used for traditional close reading.

The lack of adoption of sentiment analysis also reveals the double bind of the digital humanities community. Fast Fourier transform is a well-known method for signal extraction, and there are also accepted methods for addressing its weaknesses. For those coming from fields in which these kinds of methods are widely used, each tool is understood to be imperfect but these imperfections don't necessarily invalidate the tool. Still, for digital humanists, it is often hard to disentangle which critiques of a particular tool might invalidate the entire approach and which are only difficulties that need to be taken into consideration.

The last impediment to adoption has probably been the fact that Jockers's Syuzhet was written in R, a programming language widely used in statistics but less widely employed by potential digital humanists. In contrast to Python, arguably the most popular programming language and among the top three languages overall, R is very rarely taught in computer science and relatively unknown outside statistical and scientific applications. Currently the three most popular programming languages, according to the GitHub repo statistics compiled by GitHut on January 21, 2022, are Python (17.9 percent, up 1.4 percent from the previous year), JavaScript (14.1 percent, down 4.7 percent from the previous year), and Java (12.2 percent, up 0.66 percent).[9] R ranks thirty-sixth (0.078 percent and falling). Initial forays into sentiment analysis have thus only been made by a relatively small group of digital humanities scholars comfortable coding in R.[10] Chun's SentimentArcs in Python is now available in low-code Jupyter notebooks and we hope this expands access to the approach.[11]

There may be one more reason the approach has likely not been adopted more widely, namely its use in industry and finance. Charges of neoliberalism have been leveled at the digital humanities, and here we see the conundrum of using a method that has widespread applications for capitalist consumerism. On one hand, literary critics could consider themselves lucky: we now have at our disposal tools that were sometimes very costly to create – especially the AI transformer models. Their development was spurred by potential applications in fields with high-value payoff. Should we repurpose this approach for our own ends? Jon Chun and I believe the answer is yes.

---

[9] GitHut 2.0 https://madnight.github.io/githut/#/pull)requests/2021/4
[10] See Lei Lei and Dilin Liu's *Conducting Sentiment Analysis* for a recent example.
[11] SentimentArcs offers rpy2 access to Syuzhet and SentimentR as part of its ensemble.

1.4 Affect or Emotion? The Ethics of Quantifying Human Sentiment

Jon Chun and I call the arc that sentiment analysis surfaces a sentiment arc while others call it an emotional arc. However, there is quite a bit of confusion over affect, emotion, and sentiment, so it's worth clarifying. Sentiment analysis is not really emotion analysis. It would be easier to understand the method in light of how we now understand affect. Silvan Tomkins first described the main types of affect, which can be identified even in young babies. The experience is typified according to two factors – intensity and valence. These are the same two categories that we use to graph our sentiment analysis: (a) intensity according to the y-axis (proportional to the distance from the neutral middle line) and (b) valence (directionally upward/positive or downward/negative). What the sentiment arc really tells us, therefore, is how the intensity and valence of emotion evolve over time. When a peak is very positive, we know its intensity and valence, but not the specific emotion like joy or love, for example.

Affect theory traditionally stresses understanding certain human responses – often captured in bodily gestures or expressions – that lie outside of complex, interpretative, emotional responses to the world.[12] To the extent that affective responses can seem to preserve the unique quality of individual response prior to the overlay of all kinds of conceptual ways of making sense of the experience, affect theory has encouraged us to think about a certain level of experience before it is easily quantified or translated. Although sentiment analysis does quantify, there are similarities in the lack of translation or interpretation. On one hand, it offers us something that brings together the inchoate and often fragmentary nature of affect into a more integrated state in which various valences and intensities are connected. On the other hand, it's not "interpreted" in terms of more complex emotions.

Although people often use the words "emotion" and "affect" interchangeably, "emotion" is often used to describe these more complex responses to experiences and to describe an experience once it has been interpreted. An approach that works on this other interpretative level is called emotion analysis. Drawing on a variety of ways of classifying emotions under larger categories (joy, sadness, etc.), emotion analysis offers a different way of describing a particular text by classifying emotions into categories. While seemingly more granular, this technique is nonetheless somewhat general since all emotions are categorized into a fairly small number of bins. Our early work on *To the Lighthouse* explored this approach, but my sense is that these categories are easier for the reader to glean from a simple reading of the text. SentimentArcs,

---

[12] See Kurt Cavender et al. (2016) for an attempt to surface affect using a supervised learning model that relies on tagged data.

on the other hand, helps visualize an aspect of the reading experience that, up until now, has been harder for readers to visualize.

Another implementation of the classification approach to emotion has been used to assess characters based on personality traits.[13] Again, my sense is that literary scholars will not find this kind of approach helpful since it may seem fairly reductive. Moreover, printed words are often far too sparse for natural language processing (NLP) models to accurately reconstruct the many facets of complex personality. It's possible, however, that both of these classification approaches might be helpful for students in creative writing.

For better or worse, however, the goal of much of affective computing, which employs AI to detect human emotion, is to translate the many complex "affects" of our behavior into easily interpretable "emotions." Perhaps the most interesting takeaway from this approach is that when the many small, independent, and seemingly insignificant affective responses like word choice, speech pattern, vocal pitch, speaking rate, facial expression, and body language are taken as part of a holistic complex response, they become more interpretable. While a single affective gesture may remain opaque, it becomes less so when viewed together with many other affective responses. Many will no doubt find it dismaying that affect lends itself to quantification. While employing sentiment analysis on texts is less fraught ethically, it's worth pointing out that affective AI holds the potential to be used in many harmful ways.

Kate Crawford, in her recent book *The Atlas of AI*, raises important questions about how successful affective AI can be given that the classification of emotions relies on psychological studies, many of which have been called into question. It is quite possible that our theories of emotion are wrong: they're just models, after all. While some argue for an approach that dovetails with psychological theories (Kim and Klinger, 2018), it's important to understand that psychological theories are also models.

For better or for worse, the trend in much of AI studies is to work on creating tools that work, rather than trying to create tools that align with current psychological theory. Sentiment analysis as we employ it here does not rely on theories that classify and interpret emotions (though it does rely on a simpler model of affect).

As we in digital humanities move forward it's important to distinguish between approaches that are deployed on the level of texts and may yield

---

[13] See Kim and Klinger (2018) for an excellent comparison of the approaches and Kim, Pado, and Klinger (2017) for an application of emotion analysis to literature. Assessment of personality traits using a variety of methods (Myers-Briggs, The Big 5) is often used on Twitter data. For recent examples, see Barid et al. (2021) and Kaushal et al. (2021).

great research benefits, like sentiment analysis, and methods that work to try to model, predict, and perhaps even shape human behavior, like affective AI. Those who work in affect studies have legitimate fears about the quantification of human experience. How are we classifying emotions and for whom? Moreover, to what extent do these approaches exhibit racial and gender biases? (Kiritchenko and Mohammad, 2018). It is worth stressing that sentiment analysis of narrative requires a human-in-the-loop to oversee the analysis at all times. It says nothing about our emotional or affective experience of reading, and we reserve the qualitative analysis of the readerly experience to the human critic.

1.5 Sentiment Arc, not Story Arc

Jockers named the tool he developed Syuzhet and released it as an R library under the GPL-3 open-source license GPL-3 in 2015. There are many other tools for sentiment analysis, as I will discuss in a moment, but here I begin with Syuzhet because its name highlights certain aspects of the approach that are key for understanding how it models narrative. The distinction between two different aspects of narrative, discourse and story, or *syuzhet* and *fabula*, was first articulated by the Russian formalists Vladmir Propp and Viktor Shklovsky. While story or *fabula* refers to the chronological events within the actual story, *syuzhet* or discourse refers to time according to the way in which the narrative is presented. Sometimes discourse or *syuzhet* presents the chronology of the story out of sequence. A good example would be a novel that contains flashbacks or prolepses. While scholars often refer to this discursive aspect of *syuzhet* as "plot," many readers are more likely to think of the plot as the actions within the story time if we were to place them on a chronological timeline: in other words, *fabula*.

Syuzhet is aptly named since it graphs only discursive time and not the actual temporal sequence of events as they occur within the story. Actions can be told out of order, and it's this *syuzhet* that we're seeing when we graph the shape of the story. Sentiment analysis surfaces the shape of the narrative discourse, not the shape of the actual story time if we were to sequence events in chronological order – *fabula*.

This is just one reason it's important to emphasize, as scholars like Reagan do, that what we're graphing is better described as an emotional arc as opposed to a plot arc. We're not modeling the actual sequence of events or actions as they occurred within the story time. Rather, we're plotting the language of emotion or, more precisely, sentiment. Plot, although it often correlates with *syuzhet*, is only indirectly surfaced using the method, and when the events are presented out of order, it is less likely to correlate with plot unless we consider plot from the authorial standpoint only – how the author has "plotted" events in a particular sequence.

In a fairly straightforward narrative without unusual temporal sequencing, one might expect the actions of the novel to track quite well with emotions of a character as they find happiness or misery. But many times, as we'll see, there is much less correlation between plot and the emotion of a character. This is true if the sequence of events is presented out of order. But it is also the case if the language of sentiment follows different characters, including characters who are tangential to the plotline. Finally, one could imagine a *syuzhet* that surfaces a language of sentiment that is entirely different from the emotions of the characters, pertaining more to the language of a narrator or even the authorial choice of description. Syuzhet can thus surface a pattern that is quite distinct from plot, as will occur in many of the examples that will be discussed.

The shapes of stories that we're able to graph look like Vonnegut's graph and do sometimes track the protagonist's misery and good fortune, but not always. In the case of the Cinderella story, if the tale is told through the eyes of Cinderella, we might expect the plot to track quite closely with the sentiment arc. But if the tale were told through multiple characters' perspectives that included the step-mother and the stepsisters, for example, one could imagine a very different sentiment arc. A retelling of Cinderella that started at the ball and then flashed back to the beginning would also yield a quite different pattern. While Vonnegut emphasizes plot, therefore, Syuzhet allows us to consider plot only indirectly, and through two proxies: a language of sentiment and discourse time, not story time. Plot sometimes correlates with the sentiment arc, but doesn't always, and the extent to which they correlate will depend on the narrative.

Once we can computationally graph plot – a task many are working toward – we should be able to ascertain more clearly what this correlation between plot and sentiment arc looks like for each narrative. For now, it's worth stressing that sentiment arc complicates the simple adoption of story arcs referenced earlier since story arcs tend to be concerned with a sequence of events and the attendant emotional experiences, whereas a writer could put these events in an entirely different order and still achieve a sentiment arc that we might term "Rags to riches" or "Cinderella."

This insight is quite liberating from a creative writing perspective since many times writers can agonize over the order in which to present events. I've experimented with graphing students' drafts of novels in a story lab creative writing class and found that it can be freeing for writers to understand that they can place events in nonchronological order and still create a sentiment arc that is quite compelling. In cases like these I encourage them to think first of the sentiment arc and only secondarily about the story arc.

This suggestion might not seem as radical as it appears at first glance. Jonathan Culler points out that we tend to think of story time as the original chronological time, which is then "rearranged" in narrative time, sometimes out of order, but other times not. But, as he argues, there's no reason not to suggest the opposite hierarchy, in which discursive time or the writing of the story happens first and the rearrangement of the events into the plot or chronological story time happens only afterward through our mental representations. Syuzhet gives some credence to Culler's insight since, in fact, the story shapes that are shared across stories exist at this discursive, *syuzhet* level. In terms of the simple shape of the sentiment arc, the discourse is primary.

It may also help explain why stories can work so effectively even as the sequence of events is distorted through various flashbacks or flash-forwards. As we will see, this may explain why modernists and postmodernists can perform radical experiments with temporal sequence and still write novels that, at some fundamental level, feel like novels. Experimental stories of this nature may be less experimental than we think since their sentiment arcs can actually be very similar to the shapes of more traditional stories.

It may come as a surprise that sentiment is easier to graph than plot, so it's worth delving a bit more deeply into why this is so. It's fairly trivial to have a computer locate verbs and filter those verbs to exclude those less indicative of events – for example, "said" and "thought." One could easily create a representation of this sequence. However, one still wouldn't have the kind of plot sequence first described by Propp. It remains a challenge to group these discrete linguistic elements into basic atomic events because, in fact, many of the verbs selected, even with a good filter, will not identify the verbs key to plot advancement. Even harder is the task of grouping words into slightly longer scenes that we might term a "beat." This is, however, a field of research that is very active and we can expect advances soon.

What seems to be a bug of sentiment analysis – the inability to directly graph plot – might actually be a feature, however, since it draws our attention to the emotional engine of narrative, the way that the language of sentiment, independently of events, exhibits an underlying structure. If narratologists had designed the method from the outset, we might have started from the premise that the plot forms the shape of the story and then tried to create a program that surfaced a structure by graphing these plot events. Instead, what the approach shows us is something that we didn't think to look for.

The presence of this sentiment arc is in itself quite astonishing and raises the question of whether sentiment forms a much more fundamental element of narrative than previously thought. We've understood the crucial role of emotion since Aristotle first articulated it in his *Poetics* and writers since then – most notably Tolstoy in *What Is Art?* – have affirmed the role of emotion in art. Tolstoy argues that the communication of feeling is necessary to art and that communication is successful only if the audience feels the emotion. Still, until recently, the majority of approaches that have focused on the shape of stories have focused on plot.

It's also fascinating to realize that storytellers, whether consciously or unconsciously, often seem able to create this rise and fall in the language of sentiment, a pattern that is not always consciously available to the reader but that a computer can surface with a fairly simple tool. The sentiment arc shows us the ways in which a language of emotion rises and falls over the time of the story's telling without necessarily representing the actual events of the story.

So how does the computer manage to graph something as fuzzy as emotion? The technique is relatively simple. The first research in the field with tools like Syuzhet relied on a dictionary or lexicon of words. In the case of Syuzhet, several dictionaries are combined, normalized, and augmented. This robustness often gives Syuzhet an advantage over other lexicons in graphing novels, which tend to exhibit high linguistic diversity. Within other narrower applications – for example, sentiment analysis of customer reviews or financial industry outlooks – smaller specialized lexicons perform quite well.

Each word, phrase, sentence, or review in a sentiment analysis dictionary or labeled training set is assigned a sentiment valence within some range of positive and negative extremes. These sentiment values can be integers $(0,1)$, floating point numbers (-1.0 to $+1.0$ or 0.0 to 5.0), or labels ("positive," "neutral," "negative," or 1–5 stars). Whatever the form, these sentiment values are typically standardized with a common range (e.g. -1.0 to $+1.0$) for consistency and comparisons across trained models. This method is especially useful in cases when data are sparse – tweets, for example. For the complexity of a narrative, however, we're more interested in dictionaries that have finer granular levels of sentiment. This is because we want to discern the nuance in different gradations of valence. We'd like to know whether a word is very positive or slightly positive, very negative or slightly negative. We want to distinguish between words like abhor, hate, dislike, indifferent, like, love, and adore. We favor fine-grained approaches that allow more detailed comparisons at a smaller scale.[14] Aggregating these values over sentences or other units of text can produce the kind of unique narrative shape we seek.[15]

---

[14] There are some exceptions to these simple categories, most notably Stanza, which calculates sentiment differently.

[15] This method relies on the central limit theorem (CLT) to produce a smooth normal distribution of sentiments. The transformation to a normal statistical distribution enables a fine-grained partition of sentiment values over the time series and the course of the corpus.

The computer uses the lexicon to assign scores to words over time and tracks the narrative as the language rises and falls according to the valence and intensity of words. It does not, of course, graph happiness or misery directly and it can include far more nuanced emotions than misery and good fortune. This much more nuanced language, although more varied than happy and sad, does seem often to correspond to those moments of good fortune and bad fortune described by Vonnegut.

At this point a wide variety of lexicons are available and we have experimented with those available to us. Rinker's tool, sentimentR, incorporates heuristics – intensification and negation – and allows us to incorporate multiple lexicons, including Syuzhet, offering the strengths of qualification with an expansive dictionary. In addition to these lexical and heuristic approaches, there are three other families of models: traditional ML models, deep neural nets (DNNs), and transformer models.

Technically, both DNNs and transformers are AI representation-learning models and are able to take into account some aspects of context and multivalent linguistic use. But transformers have an attention mechanism that can make long-range associations necessary for understanding and generating coherent narratives and are so large that their qualitative differences warrant allocating them to their own class. Transformers are trained on vast quantities of language at the cost of millions of US dollars and have quickly captured many top spots in NLP task competitions. For this reason these models are usually deemed superior to the simpler lexical models because their size and complexity enable the neural models to capture pragmatics and semantics as well as syntax. For example, simple lexical and embedded vector sentiment models cannot disentangle polysemous words in which one word can have different meanings in different linguistic contexts (e.g. wicked smart or bad ass). While a simple lexical model relies on the human assignment of a value to a particular word, that assignment may be incorrect for a word that might be used quite differently in different cultural contexts or time periods.

In the majority of applications in industry, language use is relatively straightforward. Zipf's law, as it was originally formulated in quantitative linguistics, articulates the "lazy" aspect of most language use. For this reason simple dictionaries or lexicons of words can often capture the vast majority of linguistic use fairly well. Whether it's tweets (Mohammad, Bravo-Marquez, Salameh, and Kiritchenko, 2018) or movie reviews, complicated language and unusual word choice are not common, and straightforward approaches capture most semantic information in the majority of cases. It's actually surprising that these simpler tools work so well so often.

Lexical model coverage is relatively sparse, with most dictionaries number-ing from a few hundred tokens up to ten or twenty thousand. Compare this to the billions of word tokens used to train transformer models to learn many levels of statistical relationship between words and syntax, including the semantics around sentiment. These AI models can even learn implicit biases in training language to include cultural values, writing style, humor, and irony. Moreover, the more the training sets diverge from language in the narrative in question, the more likely the model will be inaccurate. Of course, lexical approaches may also inject human or cultural bias in the assigning of sentiment to a particular word, and they can also diverge from the usage in a particular narrative context.

Lexical and heuristic models offer advantages of both speed and explain-ability. Machine learning models also offer some of these advantages and can be fine-tuned on specialized data sets like financial analysis for higher per-formance within narrower domains. Representation models can incorporate more nuance and subtlety in the use of any particular word, but they are slower, require more compute power, and offer less explainability. While simpler lexical models do not take into account complex usage to the same degree, they can easily be inspected and even modified to account for the lexical specificity of the corpus. Large language transformer models, on the other hand, are largely black boxes – while one can investigate peaks and cruxes, looking inside the model to ascertain how it calculates valence is more complex (e.g. SHAP values) than the simple straightforward way one might inspect a lexicon.

In spite of the huge variety of tools and approaches, we have found that, in general, most models converge toward a common plot most of the time. One must also remember that even humans don't always agree on valence. This is measured by a metric called inter-annotator agreement. Inter-annotator agree-ment is typically lower for inherently fuzzy tasks like judging the sentiment and meaning of fiction. When assessing these tools, then, it's important to judge them against inter-annotator agreement to get a sense of how well they compare to humans performing the task. Even simpler tools like Syuzhet often do better than typical inter-annotator agreement (though not always). Moreover, while skeptics of computational approaches might wonder at the slight disagreements between models, this aspect can be seen as a benefit: multiple models offer ways to home in on points of divergence or disagreement, which can be just as informative – if not more so – than points of convergence.

As the tools improve, we should expect to see even better results alongside explainable AI that will allow us to inspect more closely the more powerful models now available. Narratives can offer some of the most complex examples of language use available to us and thus can be one of the most challenging applications for the method. For the immediate future, it's likely that a multi-model approach with a literary critic-in-the-loop will be standard practice.

1.6 Narrative Attachment

What we are discovering with sentiment analysis for narrative dovetails well with recent non-computational work in the field about how and why people engage with stories. In *Hooked: Art and Attachment* Rita Felski explores questions of engagement and emotion in a way that moves beyond mood and affect and focuses on emotion and engagement. This turn in literary studies helps us understand our engagement with narrative in a way that finds common ground with a democratized understanding of the dynamics of reading.

Felski's focus on both singularity and sociability also comports with our own research into both the unique fingerprint – the singularity – of every narrative, as well as the ways that narratives partake of larger patterns of narrative that are shared across temporal and cultural boundaries. Moreover, her interest in social networks finds an echo in the kinds of "distributed heroine" sentiment analysis can help surface. Sentiment analysis can also allow us to begin to uncover what Ben Schmidt suggests might be tensions of emotion similar to what we find in musical structure. Peaks and valleys in emotional arc surface mounting intensity of emotion, with the inflection point signaling a kind of release as the extreme emotion yields to less intense language.

2 Methods

Early critiques of the approach have turned out to be overblown. There have been other impediments to a widespread adoption of the approach for literary studies, however, foremost among them the two key issues mentioned earlier: the absence of a clear methodology and the difficulty of leveraging the approach to yield key insights about narrative. Most errors in working with sentiment analysis rely too heavily on highly smoothed curves that provide a level of abstraction quite removed from the actual novel.

If one graphs the raw data of sentiment in a narrative, it actually looks very noisy. Figure 7, for example, is what *To the Lighthouse* looks like before it is subjected to signal processing techniques. The methods used to derive a signal are the same as for many other fields. Signal extraction with various smoothing processes helps us model the more general trend upward or downward. Figure 8 shows the shapes of the story using Syuzhet. One of the smoothing methods, represented in gray, uses a simple rolling mean. Each point represents the average of the values in a sliding window. The width of the window is fixed

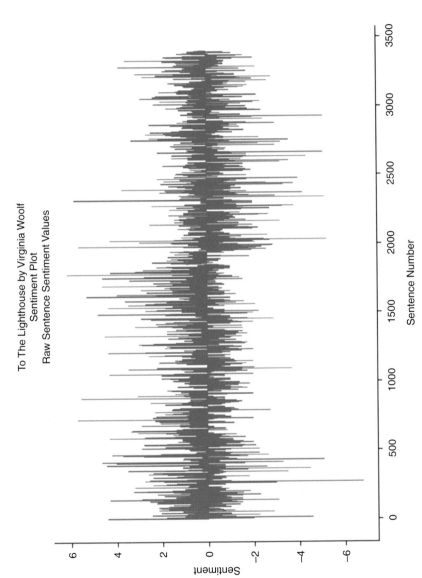

Figure 7 Raw sentiment of Woolf's *To the Lighthouse*

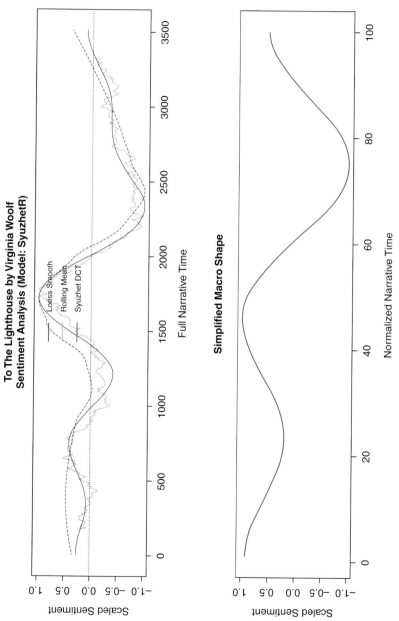

Figure 8 Smoothed sentiment of Woolf's *To the Lighthouse*

as a small percentage of the total text segment length (often 5 or 10 percent), and the window is advanced over the text segments one at a time (texts are usually segmented into individual words or sentences). This has the effect of filtering out the high-frequency, local noisy spikes to reveal low-frequency, long-term underlying trends. It is the same technique used to analyze noisy time series like financial stocks, temperature readings, and physiological signals, which fluctuate rapidly from tick to tick and yet over a longer time frame still exhibit coherent general upward and downward trends. Like sentiment arcs, Syuzhet and SentimentR can also use this same method to analyze the course of the story and extract sentiment arc from a time series of discrete sentiment values of text segments.

The red line represents the DCT, the method Jockers selected after the critique of FFT by Annie Swafford. This method uses the simple shape of a cosine function and searches for parameters that result in a curve that best fits the sequence of raw sentiment values. This method is called parametric since it uses specific parameters for the cosine function that best fit the underlying global trends rather than trying to filter out noise locally, as in the rolling window approach. One can smooth this DCT to give different levels of granularity. The simple shape is the most smoothed – essentially telling the model to look for fewer curves. While DCT can create beautifully simple arcs, its use has to be supervised carefully: it can oversimplify and distort the temporal locations of cruxes in an attempt to fit global trends dictated by model parameters.

The final method is the LOWESS (and the unweighted/less general method LOESS) in blue. Like the simple moving average, it operates on a localized sliding window basis. It doesn't presume that our data fit a global pattern and are therefore nonparametric. It offers a smoothing compromise between the intense granularity of the simple rolling mean (gray) and the global approximating approach of DCT (red). Like DCT, it attempts to fit a smooth curve based upon smoothly joined linear approximations to data points within a localized window that slides over the text in a stepwise fashion like the simple moving average seen earlier.

Note that each technique has parameters, with window size for sliding windows and fractional window size for LOWESS's specific curve-fitting function. In our case, we've found that a 10 percent sliding window over text segmented into sentences works well for many novels, but more research into hyperparameter tuning is needed. For example, segmenting Virginia Woolf's *To the Lighthouse* into 3,572 sentences with a 10 percent window of 357 sentences each results in crux points that generally comport with human interpretations. One could imagine that 5 percent might work better for unusually long novels. Moreover, the 10 percent window leaves us without much confidence near the beginning and end, and Jon Chun has experimented with ways to dilate the window size as one approaches end points to avoid clipping (5 percent at each end for a 10 percent window).

The DCT has a different method of smoothing, utilizing a model hyperparameter called the LPF low-pass filter size that is chosen by the human analyst. The LPF filter size determines how many alternating peaks and valleys the model should try to make the data fit. It filters out high-frequency noise and allows low-frequency signals to pass. No matter the method, the "smoothed" curve approximation to the underlying raw sentiment values can vary depending upon parameters to each algorithm, whether window size (rolling mean and LOWESS) or low-pass filter size (DCT).

Once one understands that DCT involves selecting the number of curves to which to fit the shape, however, one can see that smoothing methods can subject the arc to high levels of distortion. You can judge for yourself, by comparing the simple shape with the more granular shapes above it. How well does the simple shape capture the shape of the story? Smoothed to a high enough degree, one can imagine stories with fairly dissimilar shapes smoothed to appear the same.

We have found the simple moving average to provide the highest granular temporal fidelity for crux validation of a model. The abstraction of the simpler shapes gives us a much more distant sense of the narrative. You can see this most easily in the various smoothing of *To the Lighthouse* using DCT. A DCT low-pass filter of three in Figure 9 reveals a simple tragic downward curve and, intuitively, this makes sense. If we reduce the narrative to the most essential shape, it is that very steep descent. With a higher setting for the low-pass filter seen in Figures 10 and 11, one "discovers" more curves since we are essentially asking the filter to select a higher number of undulations to fit the underlying noisy series of sentiment values. Unlike the nonparametric methods of the simple moving average and the LOWESS, then, this method can change the shape of the narrative substantially because one is actually asking the model to limit the curve-fitting to a fixed number of undulations.

In a way, these various shapes make sense – as one stands at different levels of distance, one notices different "stories." At the extreme distance of Figure 9 with a filter of 3, it is pure tragedy. But with higher filters like Figures 12 and 13, one notices the emergence of the very popular double "person-in-a-hole" shape discussed earlier. The LPF7 in Figure 13 even surfaces "bestseller curves." Notice also how the boundary conditions change drastically depending on the smoothing. The beginning starts either at neutral or very positively. The ending shows even more variation, ending either very negatively, at neutral, or very positively.

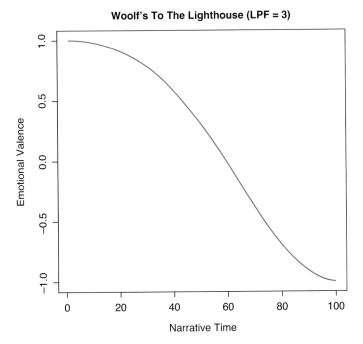

Figure 9 DCT smoothing (LPF = 3) of Woolf's *To the Lighthouse*

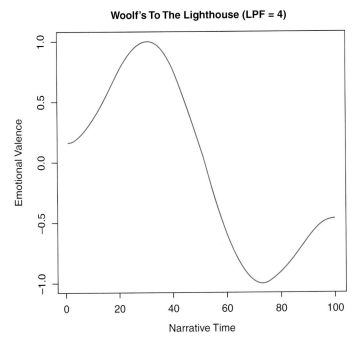

Figure 10 DCT smoothing (LPF = 4) of Woolf's *To the Lighthouse*

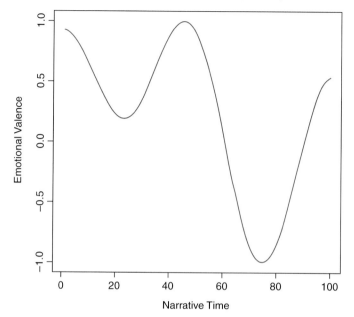

Figure 11 DCT smoothing (LPF = 5) of Woolf's *To the Lighthouse*

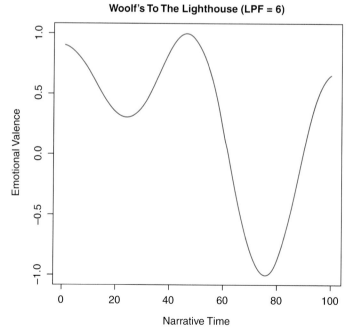

Figure 12 DCT smoothing (LPF = 6) of Woolf's *To the Lighthouse*

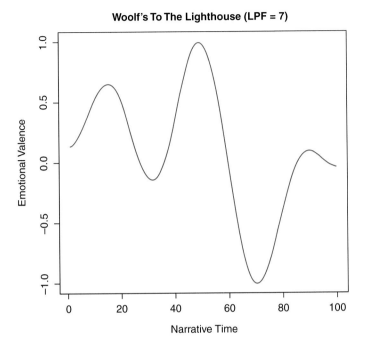

Figure 13 DCT smoothing (LPF = 7) of Woolf's *To the Lighthouse*

We recommend relying on the DCT only for the most distant sense of the basic shape of the story. Moreover, it should always be compared with the two nonparametric models and adjusted to offer a shape that most comports with the simple moving average, which is more granular. A DCT with the low-pass filter set at 5 is a good starting point, but it may not always offer the best filter. The simple shape, however, reminds us that different experiences of reading may operate at different distances from the text, and these shapes can help us begin to understand the ways in which different models help confirm – rather than deny – different emotional experiences of a single narrative.

There is a great degree of abstraction once one begins to work with the simplest of shapes. By defining the shape through the selection of a precise number of undulations, one is likely to produce shapes that are relatively similar. When Reagan's group modeled the six common shapes, they found that no actual narrative conformed exactly to their prototypical shapes. Indeed, if you look at their findings, one could just as easily argue that no two narratives are exactly alike.

Jon Chun is currently working on better ways to smooth arcs and assess fit. In particular he favors LOWESS. Since it is nonparametric, we are no longer fitting the shape to a set number of curves. Moreover, it functions at a more localized level, thus offering us a smoothing method that might better take into account particular local conditions. However, after various explorations, Chun has found that the LOWESS can still misbehave. Merely by adjusting the level of smoothing, a peak can turn into a valley and vice versa, thus yielding an entirely opposite result in localized cruxes. With SentimentArcs, he offers a LOWESS that, as with our other comparative models, yields multiple smoothings superimposed. This gives a better sense of the overall shape of the story, clearly identifying where particular smoothings diverge. In Charles Dickens's *Great Expectations*, for example, the model can reverse direction in a few places, notably, around sentences 700 and 3,000, as seen in Figure 14. In these localized places the models offer us less confidence. The multiple smoothings superimposed also show how easily different smoothings can yield crux points that move slightly along the horizontal axis. This reinforces our sense that cruxes are approximate rather than precise. Multiple smoothings allow us to better assess these discrepancies and variance.

These smoothings can still be helpful, therefore. They remind us, as with Woolf, that in spite of the curves the simplest sense of the story may be of a tragedy. In the case of Dickens, smoothing helps make apparent more basic shapes that the very granular rolling mean can make hard to ascertain. Still it's important to remember that the singular fingerprint of a narrative rarely conforms clearly to any of the six (or seven) basic shapes. While there has been much groundbreaking work on the simple shape of stories, there is still much work to be done in the realm of the many and very complex shapes of stories.

2.1 Single Models, Singular Stories

How is a particular story unique and how is its method of representing events also unique? Working with a more granular shape of the story – not its simple shape – can help us answer these questions. This more granular shape offers less traction for comparing shapes across stories. On the other hand, it offers unique peaks and valleys, easily located in the text, to analyze and validate models against human understanding. This allows us to start with what is unique and individual and it further emphasizes that the more smoothed graphs – which look more like other stories – are always "wrong" but, depending on one's goal, can be useful, especially for general comparison.

For those of us interested in this unique aspect of a particular narrative, the 10 percent rolling window (gray) in Syuzhet provides a suitable level of granularity. It offers an intermediate shape that is not as noisy as the raw signal

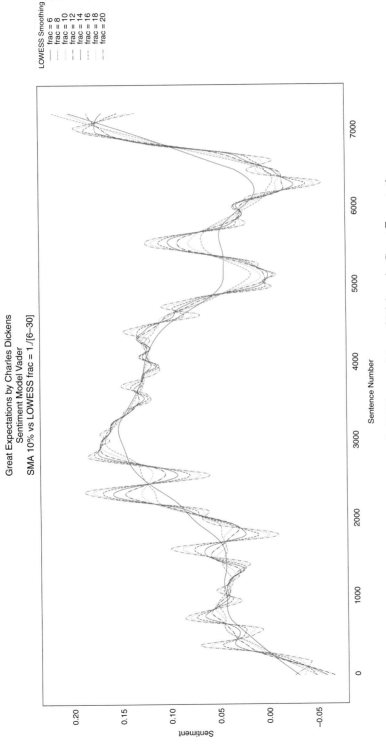

Figure 14 SMA versus LOWESS smoothing of Dickens's *Great Expectations*

but far more granular than any of the other smoothing methods. This smoothing method, moreover, allows for more precise extraction of moments of inflection when the overall trend in language shifts from rising to falling and vice versa. One way of thinking of these peaks and valleys is as the high and low points of sentiment in the text. But another way of thinking about these is as moments of transition – when the narrative, using the language of sentiment, reverses direction.

Literary critics who fear the rise of computational literary analysis are right to be wary of any method that suggests a computer can analyze the text and that all that's left for us to do is to run the algorithm and present a graph. This may be yet one more reason that many reacted negatively to Jockers's initial work. Jockers pointed out that the peaks and valleys, or the highest and lowest moments on the curves, correlate quite often with key scenes in the novel. That is, the algorithm extracted many of the passages that are typically selected for close reading.

Having graphed many novels, Jon Chun and I can affirm that a peak detection algorithm to extract the local and global minimum and maximum points in a smoothed time series works well to surface key passages most of the time. To the extent that the sentiment arc cruxes comport with sections of the text that scholars find significant, we can surmise why: those textual passages mark an inflection point in the language of sentiment. As you will see in the examples that follow, it can be just as interesting to evaluate points of inflection that surprise us. We can also explore the precise language in the passages that surround these moments, an approach that allows for a white-box as opposed to a black-box method. Moreover, when computational methods and human reading comport, this method can offer useful ways to help attune us to the language of sentiment. Even so, nothing could be further from automation than sentiment analysis of novels when exploring the unique fingerprint of a story. When working with this more individual pattern, human analysis is key throughout the entire process.

Since all models are wrong but some models are useful, the question becomes: what might this model be useful for? When Jon Chun and I began our work we had a few questions to answer. Is there a way to adapt this approach to methods of close reading, one of the most fundamental aspects of literary criticism? What are the limitations of the approach and how can we come up with research questions that leverage its strengths while avoiding its weaknesses? Finally, can the approach show us something more than what many see digital humanities to offer: the null or the obvious?

Given this critique of digital humanities, Jon Chun and I thought it best to begin with a research question that is neither null nor obvious and one that investigates just how innovative narrative form may be in modernist narrative.

Modernist novels are widely understood to highlight representations of consciousness over representations of external events. Temporal innovations also lead to many experiments with typical plotting. In *To the Lighthouse* one might summarize the plot as: Part One: They Wish to Go to the Lighthouse (but Can't); Part Two: Time Passes; Part Three: They Go to the Lighthouse. If one wanted to add a bit more granularity one could include the painter Lily and offer that her metaphorical trip to the lighthouse is the completion of her painting, which she finishes as she watches the others complete their voyage. There is, moreover, one key event – a dinner party scene presided over by the matriarch of the family, Mrs. Ramsay.

Although not much happens, you can see from that clear signal surfaced by sentiment analysis that the novel has a very strong sentiment arc and these main "events" of the story, however slight, nonetheless track with a very pronounced shape. The muted focus on events, in other words, is not mirrored in a muted arc of sentiment. On one hand, this may not surprise everyone since many modernists find enchantment in the smallest of daily events, which can provide intense emotional experience. What is striking, however, in the sentiment arc of *To the Lighthouse* is how extremely pronounced the rise and fall in the center of the narrative is. While we had a sense of this extreme intensity when we began working with the approach, I can confirm that, at least for the many novels that I have graphed, this extreme central rise and fall is unusual.

One should be cautious in comparing analysis of linguistic data to techniques developed for numeric data analysis. However, some of the more general principles of exploratory data analysis (EDA), developed by the statistician John Tukey, are helpful. In particular, Tukey emphasizes that the visualization of data and an exploration of the visual component can bring to light elements that other analytic approaches cannot. Unlike confirmatory data analysis, which is hypothesis driven, EDA holds more in common with our traditional approaches to literature. Tukey advises letting the "data speak for itself," just as we might let a novel inform how we read and analyze it.

What general impressions might we glean from this visualization? Here we introduce one of the newer state-of-the-art methods for plotting sentiment analysis, one based on a large transformer model, RoBERTa, fine-tuned on fifteen labeled sentiment training data sets. The sentence line numbers offer a way to explore each crux point and assess how well the model graphs key cruxes of the novel. As seen in Figure 15, the opening of the novel evinces a fairly choppy emotional flux as both positive and negative sentiments are described: it's unclear if the weather will be good enough to make the trip to the lighthouse, and this uncertainty is reflected in the sentiment arc. Then the novel rises in positive emotional intensity to the

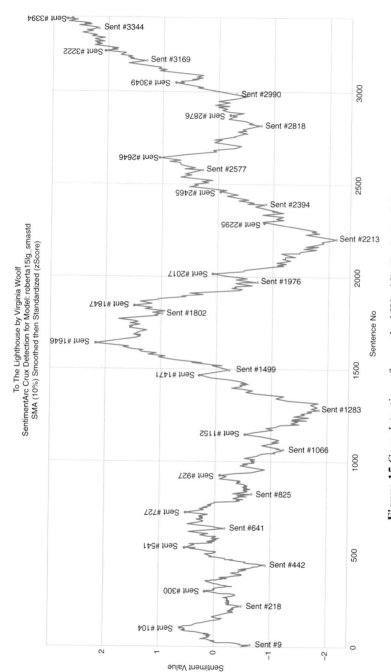

Figure 15 Crux detection of smoothed Woolf's *To the Lighthouse*

scene of the dinner party, after which it plunges again during the Time
Passes section, when several of the Ramsays die. There is a gradual rise of
positive sentiment when characters return to the summer house after the
passing of so much time, and Lily, the painter, tries once again to finish her
painting. Both Lily and the Ramsay children experience frustration during
the trip to the lighthouse, but the novel builds toward a more positive
resolution as Lily finishes her painting and the Ramsays finally approach
the lighthouse.

On the first pass of EDA, therefore, we can conclude that the opening of the
novel has a fairly spiked level of affective flux, followed by a much stronger
sentiment arc in the middle when the narrative continues in one direction for
a longer period of time. The final section shows some of the same spiked flux as
the beginning but nonetheless evinces a clearer upward movement.

Jon Chun and I call this level of analysis "middle reading" because it focuses
on the level of the novel rather than the larger corpora of many novels used for
distant reading.[16] On the most fundamental level, what it offers is a sense of how
these various moments in the novel relate to each other in terms of the language
of sentiment. It also gives us a sense that there is an underlying structure to the
novel – sometimes more pronounced, other times less – that correlates loosely
with plot but is more precisely indicative of a language of affect that carries us
through the novel.

On one hand, it offers us something that can be somewhat intuited: it is not
terribly surprising to find that the dinner party offers a very strong emotional

---

[16] In the following sections it will become clearer how the "middle" aspect of middle reading works
on multiple levels. For several years now Jon Chun and I have focused on approaches like this
that we term "middle reading." This is in contrast to the "close reading" of short text passages –
traditionally the focus of human literary scholars – and the automated "distant reading" approach
introduced by Moretti that uses computational algorithms to surface underlying statistical
patterns from hundreds or even thousands of novels. "Middle reading" focuses on texts at the
scale where narrative is commonly experienced as most meaningful to humans: a single novel,
a movie script, a comic book series, or a newspaper topic over time. At this scale the size of the
text is too sparse for the statistical ML algorithms used in "distant reading" and too complex for
a human to comprehensively analyze using close reading alone. Of course the term "middle
reading" has been used to describe different phenomena across different fields both before and
after we formally introduced it as our approach to sentiment analysis research (Elkins and Chun,
2019). It has never been defined like this, however, or explicitly applied to the merging of AI/ML
techniques and literary criticism. Historians have used the term to refer to the interpretive
analysis between qualitative and quantitative historical sources (Rosenthal); linguists have
used the term to describe an intermediate level of syntactic analysis (Jones); some digital
humanist have used the term to describe an analysis between "close" and "distant" reading,
but without concrete examples or methodology (Bugg) (Mulholland). Our contribution is to
build upon initial efforts by others to work on the level of a single novel, formalizing the term and
object of study, systematizing methodologies across multiple models (sentiment, topic modeling,
etc.) and using advances in state-of-the-art large language models to create more accurate results
and solve the sparsity problem that sometimes arises as text corpora shrink.

peak and the Time Passing section an emotional valley. In this case one can conclude that in spite of so little "plot," Woolf creates a very pronounced sentiment arc that can create a very compelling reading experience in spite of so little happening.

Of course not everyone finds the novel emotionally compelling, and to the extent that readerly experiences differ, this middle reading can offer clues as to divergent reading experiences. One interesting aspect of what EDA of *To the Lighthouse* shows us is that the sentiment arc is indeed noisier near the beginning of the narrative. The opening pages of the novel are filled with a great deal of emotional ambivalence and with great variation in the ups and downs.

The character, Lily, finds herself asking how she should feel about people, and her language involves a multitude of emotions, many contradictory. While it will not always be the case that the novel thematically mirrors the emotional spiked nature of the graph, there is an astonishing symmetry between the ways in which the sentiment arc mirrors the emotional ambivalence thematically described. Lily is trying to ascertain a strong emotional signal out of the complex signals from others:

> Standing now, apparently transfixed, by the pear tree, impressions poured in upon her of those two men, and to follow her thought was like following a voice which speaks too quickly to be taken down by one's pencil, and the voice was her own voice saying without prompting undeniable, everlasting, contradictory things.

How should she feel about people, who embody so many different contradictions and in turn produce so many contradictory emotions in her own assessment of them?[17] We see this same philosophical sense of the world embodied in the beginning narrative structure, which moves up and down rather than embarking on a clear emotional trajectory that holds its course.

Woolf is well known for innovations in her language, in particular for an attention to "moments of being" that hold more in common with some poetic forms than with narrative. The beginning section of the narrative also seems to suggest a quite different approach to narrative, one that innovates by postponing the very strong sentiment arc that will appear later in the novel. Readers who

---

[17] It would be highly artificial to consult bound copies of works and insert traditional citations when this approach relies on a digital text without page numbers. I believe it's worth highlighting this digital aspect of the process and not camouflaging it behind traditional citation structure. Also, I refrain from adding scholarly citations except when absolutely necessary. Integrating this approach with more traditional scholarship is an important next step and will require far more space than I am allowed here. Still many of these arcs have been subject to scholarly debate through panel presentations at the Modernist Studies Association, the Modern Language Association, and the International Society for the Study of Narrative. I am indebted to my fellow panelists, presiders, and audience members for our lively and insightful discussions.

think of the beginning of this narrative as more poetic may be right, then, since it demonstrates less of a clear narrative sentiment arc. Midway through the novel, however, the sentiment arc offers us longer periods of travel in one direction: the climax of the dinner party at midpoint is followed by a tragic plunge with the onset of the war and subsequent deaths of key characters. Can a plotless novel show a strong underlying structure? Yes. Do segments of Woolf's narrative surface a less clear sentiment arc? Yes, as well.

2.2 Ensemble Models

So far we have explored one of the simplest lexical models, Syuzhet, and one of the most complex AI models, RoBERTa. Jon Chun and I have worked with more than thirty sentiment models from simple lexical dictionaries to state-of-the-art transformers, and the task of recommending one particular model over another presents multiple challenges. On one hand, tools today may quickly be replaced by newer tools tomorrow. Equally perplexing, however, is a genre – narrative – whose diversity of language and form is dizzying. Tools that work well for one novel do not work equally well for another.[18] While it's easy to assume that the newest models, like RoBERTa, will always work best, this has not proven to be our experience (Chun, 2021). Chun's SentimentArcs provides an easy way to use an ensemble of models to assess optimal pairing of a specific novel to the most performant model in the ensemble. It also offers quantitative methods of determining how divergent the various models are. Although a greater number of models that agree is evidence of a stronger signal in general, it can always be the case that a divergent model – an outlier – could be more accurate and this possibility, although less likely, should be kept in mind.

Much of what follows focuses on two aspects of sentiment analysis for narrative: developing methods that work well regardless of tool, and showing ways in which an ensemble method that leverages multiple models of sentiment analysis is also a recommended approach for the near future. When working with different models, it can seem as though each model is like a different "reader" with a distinct view of the novel. As in a community of readers, the ensemble approach generates a synthetic ground truth utilizing the wisdom of crowds approach in which more perspectives are usually better. Even with a multi-model approach, however, it's critical to rely on human judgment to assess which models are best and where they fail.

For those new to sentiment analysis, it's a good strategy to begin with a few simple models to get a sense of the approach. Given the need to fit

---

[18] SentimentArcs offers the same joint optimization method for a wide variety of texts, from tweets to newspaper articles, judicial decisions to political speeches.

model to narrative, however, an ensemble method is useful once one has practiced using the simplest models. As Chun writes, "the suggested approach is to start with the ensemble baseline to seek a baseline sentiment arc. Then, to seek more subtle features and anomalies, progressively study narratives further from the consensus" (2021). We have found a few models to be less accurate for the novels we have analyzed, but it is possible they will be useful for certain narratives, and several of them work well with other kinds of text (e.g. movies, tweets, financial filings) because they have been trained on language specific to that genre. While these outliers usually suggest weaker signals, it's always possible anomalous behavior can be revealing of unusual textual features. Figure 16 is an ensemble model of *To the Lighthouse* with thirty-four models and their mean. For those not familiar with signal processing, it's important to stress that this level of agreement is not random, and it's safe to say that we have a fairly strong signal, especially given such a fuzzy data set as a novel.

Another way to get a better sense of sentiment arc is to explore interclass coherence by comparing the different families of models. When choosing to compare models, we recommended considering both family of model as well as divergence, as seen on a heatmap, to gain a broader sense of possible points of contention as well as points of agreement. There are a few cautions regarding coherence. We have found that the more sophisticated models are often more variable as a family (e.g. transformers) and can stand out from more coherent lexical models that may share a common core vocabulary. In terms of comparison, there is another aspect to note: these various tools all use different scales. While SentimentArcs standardizes models to facilitate direct comparison, some caution is warranted in assessing the intensity of the peaks and valleys, which can be affected by unusually large and or numerous outliers.

A multi-model approach reinforces our sense that the beginning of the narrative is "noisy" with quick shifts in the change of direction. The central peak holds strong with some variation directly on either side. A common way of dealing with model discrepancies when working with numeric data is to work with the mean or average, which is shown as the dark line in Figure 16.

In this instance the models comport well, and it's often best to work with the lexical and heuristic models because of their explainability. We confirm the choice with a quick look at these models in comparison to the full ensemble seen in Figure 17. In later case studies I will use a single model or a mean of explainable models when the models conform well. It is less helpful, however, when there is a fair amount of divergence. In cases like these it's possible that some models may work better for a particular author, time period, or genre, and that by finding the mean we actually overlook the models that offer the best fit.

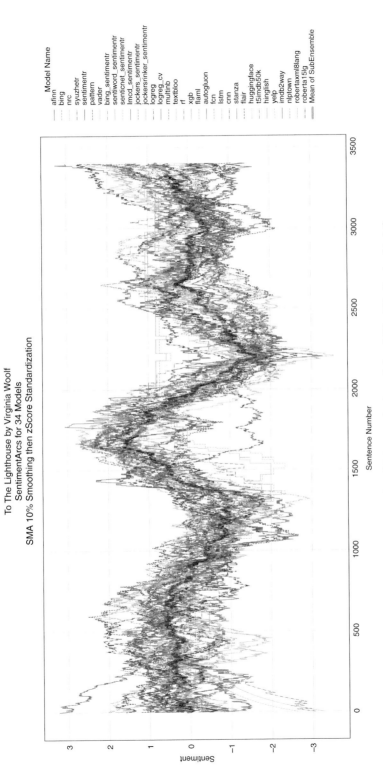

Figure 16 Ensemble of 34 smoothed models of Woolf's *To the Lighthouse*

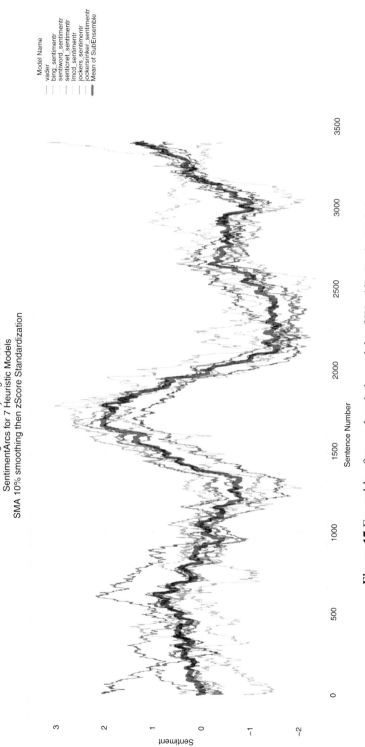

Figure 17 Ensemble of seven heuristic models of Woolf's *To the Lighthouse*

For this reason, until we have a more precise sense about which models work best for which corpora, and absent an AI model that works well for all novels in all circumstances, we advocate a method that we call clustered close reading. Clustered close reading offers us one way of leveraging the strengths of an ensemble method. In a more typical data science environment, ensemble methods often employ a consensus method that favors those models that agree. Because the narratives we work with often push the limits of our method, however, it's prudent to give more weight to methods that agree, but to consider the possibility that an outlier may offer a better method of modeling a particular narrative.

2.3 Clustered Close Reading

Clustered close reading is a method of comparing different families of models by examining clusters of key peaks and valleys. With this ensemble method, we focus first on the major peaks and valleys in order to narrow our search space. Sometimes different model cruxes are clustered quite closely. At other times they diverge more widely. In either case, the critic-in-the-loop can validate how well the models perform and which are more accurate.

For a case study, I turn again to *To the Lighthouse*. We would expect cruxes to be clustered quite closely, given our earlier EDA of the ensemble. A note of caution is in order before we continue. Because of slight variations in each model, some cruxes may not be extracted (i.e. not be marked by a line number) if there is another crux in close proximity. It's important to inspect models visually since the graphs will surface peaks and valleys that may be unmarked (depending on the sliding window) but that are similar to those marked in a different model.

Crux detection is an active area of research and SentimentArcs will soon be updated with a novel method for extracting peaks customized for the challenges that sentiment time series present. For that reason results may differ very slightly from our results here, but not significantly so. For our clusters we select a wide range of models by drawing from each family: lexical (Syuzhet), heuristics (VADER, SentimentR), traditional ML (TextBlob), DNNs (of the CNN/LSTM variety, like FLAIR and Stanza), and transformer (RoBERTa). The vast majority of the models converge, so the tendency should be to consider the outlier results in this broader context.

We start with the central peak of the novel. Here we see general comportment of models with minor differences. Using the SMA, Table 1 shows the average sentence line of the peak for each model.

Table 1 Central peak in *To The Lighthouse* by V. Woolf

Model Name	Sentence Number
Syuzhet.R	1649
SentimentR	1646
VADER	1650
Stanza	1655
TextBlob	1668
FLAIR	1649
RoBERTa	1646

Syuzhet.R, SentimentR, and VADER are all fairly similar tools, so we would expect findings to be similar, and they are. For this peak of the novel inflection points differ by at most a sentence (1649–1650). The tightest cluster includes these models along with RoBERTa (1646) and FLAIR (1649). We start with this tightest cluster before exploring our outliers, Stanza (1655) and TextBlob (1668):

> So she saw them; she heard them; but whatever they said had also this quality, as if what they said was like the movement of a trout when, at the same time, one can see the ripple and the gravel, something to the right, something to the left; and the whole is held together; for whereas in active life she would be netting and separating one thing from another; she would be saying she liked the Waverly novels or had not read them; she would be urging herself forward; now she said nothing (1646). For the moment, she hung suspended.
>
> "Ah, but how long do you think it'll last?" said somebody. It was as if she had antennae trembling out from her, which, intercepting certain sentences, forced them upon her attention (1649). This was one of them (1650).

Most models locate the averaged peak during this moment of the dinner party scene when there is a distinct phase transition as the room takes on a different quality, when "the whole is held together." Stanza locates the crux a few sentences later, when William Bankes asks "Who could tell what was going to last – in literature or indeed in anything else?" before concluding, "Let us enjoy what we do enjoy" (1655). TextBlob, the outlier in this cluster, finds the moment falling even a dozen sentences later, when Paul Rayley asserts of some of the books he had read as a boy: "They lasted" (1668). We can see a bit more emotional ambivalence about the duration of happiness in these outlier models, but they also do a good job picking up the conclusion of positivity: "Let us enjoy what we do enjoy" and "They lasted." It's hard not to side with the majority of the models as highlighting the highest moment in the early part of the scene.

However, it's also possible to see the scene as continuing as a sort of a plateau to include the outliers before a clear downward turn.

We turn now to anomaly detection and a consideration of model divergence. After this extended scene, Syuzhet begins an almost immediate downward descent while other models locate a second peak after a brief dip. The slight dip occurs during a scene when Mrs. Ramsay leaves the dinner party, worries about her husband, and tries to comfort her son James, who is scared by a skull hanging on the bedroom wall. In some models the next, second peak is even higher than the first that we just examined, as can be seen in Table 2. Those that locate it higher are marked by an asterisk.

Let's validate this second clustered peak, which occurs in the scene after the dinner party, when Mr. and Mrs. Ramsay are reading together. Are some models right to surface it? And might it rise even higher than the dinner party scene? Indeed some critics have told me they find this second peak to be more central. It offers a slightly more ambivalent moment, however, since Mr. and Mrs. Ramsay are reading different texts and their thoughts and emotions diverge somewhat. One's thoughts on how "positive" this moment (and even this marriage) may be could easily influence how one reads the moment. Nonetheless, it's definitely the case that this is the last peak – however intense – before the novel descends into a very profound valley.

Let's turn now to a clustered close reading of one of the central valleys of the novel as seen in Table 3. All of the models except one locate the major valley after the dinner scene within a thirteen-line window (2200–2213) with the exception of one outlier (Stanza, 2246).

After time has passed, some of the visitors return to the island and the Ramsays are preparing for the trip to the lighthouse. Questions about what to send to the

Table 2 Peak after dinner scene in *To The Lighthouse* by V. Woolf

Model Name	Sentence Number (V)alley and (P)eak
Syuzhet.R	None with 5 percent peak detection Window
SentimentR	1174 (V) 1847 (P)
Vader	1805 (V) 1848 (P)
Stanza	1795 (V) 1905 (P)*
TextBlob	1759 (V) 1842 (P) *
FLAIR	1806 (V) 1865 (P)
RoBERTa	1802 (V) 1847 (P) *

* Higher

Table 3 First major valley after dinner
scene in *To The Lighthouse* by V. Woolf

Model Name	Sentence Number
Syuzhet.R	2200
SentimentR	2213
VADER*	2205
Stanza	2246
TextBlob*	2200
FLAIR	2205
RoBERTa	2213

lighthouse give way to existential thoughts ("What does one do? Why is one sitting here, after all?") and reflection on all who have died (2205 to 2213):

> The house, the place, the morning, all seemed strangers to her. She had no attachment here, she felt, no relations with it, anything might happen, and whatever did happen, a step outside, a voice calling ("It's not in the cupboard; it's on the landing," some one cried), was a question, as if the link that usually bound things together had been cut, and they floated up here, down there, off, anyhow. How aimless it was, how chaotic, how unreal it was, she thought, looking at her empty coffee cup. Mrs. Ramsay dead; Andrew killed; Prue dead too – repeat it as she might, it roused no feeling in her.

The deaths of these characters have occurred earlier in the narrative, so it's somewhat of a surprise to realize that those are not the lowest points of the narrative. Rather, a passage that recounts a lack of emotional attachment – "she had no attachment here" – creates the strongest signal. One might hypothesize that Woolf crafts a sentiment arc beautifully by exploring contrasts between the way a text "feels" in terms of its characters, its language, and its readers. This valley calls our attention to the difference between these various modes of "feeling" in a text. Lily claims to feel no attachment. But the narrative maintains language with clear sentiment: "aimless," "chaotic," "empty," "dead," and "killed." The reader, if they have formed a narrative attachment to the characters who have died, may experience these "thoughts" with great emotion.

A second question arises, however, this one similar to that raised about the peak. Should we judge a valley as the lowest emotional point, or as the moment of inflection when the sentiment arc begins to rise? Viewed from the latter perspective, it makes more sense that even after the deaths of several of the Ramsays, the narrative continues in a negative space for quite some time to include this later moment before beginning its rise.

Stanza, an outlier, locates the moment of inflection much later, when Lily finally begins to paint while standing in the same spot where she stood ten years ago. As yet another complication, two of the models, marked by an asterisk, agree with the earlier valley but then descend further to key scenes between Lily and Mr. Ramsay (discussing boots) and the boat trip (describing a shipwreck). These later moments suggest a certain level of "noisiness" in the language that follows the return to the summer house. It is almost as though there is an aftereffect from time passing with all its death and destruction. At the very least, some of these negatively valenced moments do suggest that it takes quite a while for the sentiment arc to turn definitively toward an upward trajectory.

There are several other areas of convergence in the novel's sentiment arcs. Virtually all of the models agree that there is a valley between lines 916 and 963. This is when Mr. and Mrs. Ramsay are walking in the garden and he worries about her looking so sad. Several models locate a trough in a wide cluster (1283, 1309, 1319, 1334). This scene is one with a character, Charles Tansley, who is disliked by other characters in the story (and very possibly, therefore, by the reader). Tansley is feeling very lonely and insists the weather will prevent a trip to the lighthouse. He then reflects on the ways in which people drift apart and concludes that social obligations are a waste of time since they distract from his work. We can see the increased divergence of the clustered approach here since clusters locate general areas, but with less precision. This is truly a "middle reading" since the cluster extends across fifty sentences. Moreover, this is yet one more instance when the language of the text and the sentiment of a particular character may diverge from readerly feeling quite significantly.

2.4 Middle Reading and the Critic-in-the-Loop

Clustered close reading leads us to a new conclusion that also holds when working with a single model. Often models cluster points of inflection across a fairly narrow range of a few sentences, as we saw in the first peak. But sometimes cruxes might range across a wider section of text, as with the last example. The size of the passage will therefore vary. Moreover, since we're dealing with a smoothing technique, all findings have a level of approximation since uneven language of sentiment will be smoothed, albeit on a fairly granular level when employing the SMA.

Thus it's important to keep in mind that the single sentence identified as the crux point should be evaluated with sentences on both sides as part of a larger point of inflection, and with the larger cluster if using an ensemble. Moreover, when working across multiple models, the size of the range of the cluster will likely determine the size of the passage considered. Sometimes a cluster constitutes a longer scene rather than the single paragraph or two typical of close reading.

The crux extractor can be adjusted to whatever size passage you like. However, we do advocate a larger-than-average passage size since the cruxes are approximate rather than precise. While in general it's fairly poor form in literary studies to include large passages since this runs counter to the "close" of close reading, in this case it is imperative. Clustered close reading thus works toward a "middle reading" by finding a "middle ground" of many models as well as by working with a slightly larger passage than is typical for close reading. Moreover, middle reading conveys the "approximate" nature of the cruxes – since they are average, it is less precise than the "close" reading of a single line. Finally, middle reading also applies to the ways in which analysis focuses on an underlying structure of a single novel, as opposed to the distant reading so common in digital humanities as a field.

Fewer models allow one to get comfortable with the process and gain an intuitive sense of how it works. Still middle reading reminds us to see a single crux as probable and to read a passage as approximate rather than definitive. With clustered close reading, we can gain confidence and precision. The more that very different models comport, the more confidence we can have in the cluster.

It's important to remember that all models are wrong, and we can see from comparing the models that there is disagreement about the peaks and valleys, as well as about the degree of intensity, which very often mirror readerly disagreement. Valleys that approach neutral can be similarly complex, a reminder that neutrality does not always mean "neutral" valence, but can rather signal emotional experiences that are ambivalent.

It's fairly easy to benchmark existing models against Amazon and Yelp reviews, as some have already done. But it's much harder to benchmark novels, although we continue to work toward this goal. Some tools will work better with some novels. Even as these models get better, however, it's probably still worth asking, how wrong are these models? Here we see the need for the critic-in-the-loop.

Were the moments identified by the computational model of *To the Lighthouse* the ones that a reader might select from the novel? For the most part, they were. When we first presented our research to my modernist scholars group, Stephen Kern insisted we had gotten all the cruxes right but had left out one.[19] This raises an interesting question. It's always useful to ask: what did the

---

[19] Many thanks are due our group led by Stephen Kern: Morris Beja, Ellen Jones, Brian McHale, William Palmer, Jim Phelan, and Jessica Prinz. I am also grateful for conversations with Sarah Copland, Adam Hammond, and Jesse Matz.

model miss? The discrepancy between the model and our own reading experience can help illuminate further insights by leveraging the critic-in-the-loop.

In this case the moment in question happens just after the dinner table scene, when Mr. and Mrs. Ramsay retreat from the party to read. As you will remember, Syuzhet – which we were using at the time – did not surface this moment. But the other models all did. Here we see a good example of why multiple models are worth comparing, as well as the need to consider what models might leave out.

Which moment – the dinner scene or this quiet moment in the marriage of the Ramsays – should be graphed higher? There the models don't agree nor, I imagine, will all readers. Finally, there are clearly cases when our affective experience will differ from the language of the narrative. However, even here, we need to be careful. I had always imagined that the mention of Mrs. Ramsay's death in brackets was poignant precisely because readerly emotion diverged so dramatically from the emotionless portrayal:

> [Mr. Ramsay, stumbling along a passage one dark morning, stretched his arms out, but Mrs. Ramsay having died rather suddenly the night before, his arms, though stretched out, remained empty.]

There is no typical language of emotion here. And yet the transformer RoBERTa maps the sentiment fairly well. It assigns the sentence a score of -0.99 out of -1. Why might this be? In spite of the lack of explicit language of emotion, there is much sentiment beyond the verb that announces her death: the stumbling, the "dark" morning, and the empty arms.

And yet, even with so much agreement between reader and model, when I've asked students to graph the sentiment arc of *To the Lighthouse*, they've often had difficulty. This may be because they have been told that the novel is plotless and experimental. Or it may be thanks to the influence of Woolf herself, who suggested that the shape of the plot was an H. And yet, when one steps back and considers many of the cruxes, they comport well with human evaluation. Here we see the possibility of a digital humanities approach that offers methods for exploring what is neither null nor obvious, the "middle reading" of the novel. What the computational model can do is often quite difficult for the reader: getting an immediate sense of the underlying shape of the story.

A human-in-the-loop, then, can assess both the inter-model agreement and the agreement between reader response and the language of the text. They can also assess the noisiness of the graph. We can return to that first EDA of *To the Lighthouse* using a single model and confirm certain larger patterns. Inter-model agreement would seem to confirm the noisy nature of parts of the sentiment arc since none of the arcs surface a stronger signal. If you examine the quick shift in up and down moments in a sawtooth pattern you can understand why. If one is a bit off in modeling this constantly shifting affect, it would be very easy to fall into an exact opposite moment, descending into a valley instead of locating a peak, for example, or vice versa. This too is useful information because it confirms the sense that the beginning is harder to graph than the midsection of the novel and that the beginning may be a bit more experimental.

One conclusion, then, is that some aspects of the method are more useful than others. When there's frequent directional change in valence, the approximate nature of the approach should give us reason to proceed with caution. Other novels, in which there is a much more gradual shift in valence, are undoubtedly easier. Woolf's novel, which exhibits so much emotional ambivalence, may be an outlier in this regard. A further useful aspect of the method is the ability to compare peaks and valleys and to determine whether more general thematic principles hold across cruxes – another aspect of a "middle" reading. In this case we find that they do. Where the sentiment arc is noisy we can see the narrative itself engages in evaluations that are highly contradictory. Where the signal is stronger, however, there is a clearer emotional focus. The peaks occur during moments of connection and beauty. At her most joyful, these moments in Woolf can feel like that moment of lightness at the top of the roller coaster as one is suspended for a brief second before changing direction. Then the sentiment arc descends into valleys that describe death and dispersion, sadness and isolation. Even though very little "happens" in the novel, the peaks and valleys show opposing moments of connection and disconnection, both between characters and between selves and world.

2.5 Whose Emotions? The Distributed Heroine

I have already touched on discrepancies between readerly emotion and the sentiment of the text. Another good example can be found in Orwell's *Animal Farm*: when the pigs gain ascendancy over the other animals the emotional arc rises even as the reader is meant to react to this rise quite differently. Here we can see that the emotional arc, as a computational approach, is quite literal, mapping the sentiment (or its absence) in the text without reference to how a reader might feel about the character(s) in question. For this reason Kim and Klinger (2018, 2019) have worked on classifying emotions for each character as a way to disentangle this element of narrative. However, this approach offers great challenges. Localizing emotion for each character may run into difficulties because of the sparseness of the linguistic data. For each scene, the number of words to ascertain a character's emotion may be quite small. Kim and Klinger take an ML approach to tackling the problem with human annotation of gesture, facial expression, and other indicators of emotion that might not be surfaced by traditional sentiment analysis.

The challenges emotion analysis presents highlight an unusual element of the practice of sentiment analysis. Once again, the approach has not been designed with our interests in mind. The question of whose emotion is ignored. A narrative might surface a sentiment arc of a single heroine, but it might just as well surface a collective sentiment arc as it does in *To the Lighthouse*.

Sentiment analysis as a method ignores who is feeling what, although researchers are actively working to align sentiment arc to character. Rather, there is a sentiment arc of the narrative that is independent at times of these character concerns and agnostic as to classification of sentiment into discrete emotional states. And yet it can offer insights in spite of and even because it does not surface what we might have looked for had we designed it solely for literary analysis. The method surfaces a language of sentiment that is independent of any particular human, whether character or reader, and independent of any theories of classification of emotion.

What might seem a weakness can actually be seen as a strength. Let's explore how Woolf, a twentieth-century writer, navigates what the literary scholar Alex Woloch (2003) identifies as a tension typical in many nineteenth-century novels. The focus on a single individual ("the one") is constantly undercut by a supporting cast so large as to draw our focus away from that individual. Woolf, as a modernist, might be seen as a writer who takes this tension to the extreme by dipping into many characters' consciousness. Is the focus of the novel Lilly or Mrs. Ramsay (or even Charles Tansley)? One dips into so many different minds that it becomes difficult to say.

What is surprising is that a single sentiment arc connects these various minds in a unified shape. One would expect the sentiment arc to appear fragmented or noisy, given so many different hero(ine)s. And yet it's not. Instead, Woolf is able to create what we term a "distributed heroine" sentiment arc. While descriptions of a story arc are likely to favor an interpretation centered around a single character – the so-called hero's journey – a middle reading of Woolf's *To the Lighthouse* offers crux points that are distributed across multiple characters.

This sentiment arc may provide a sense of cohesiveness even as key moments and experiences are distributed across a range of characters. The cruxes form a shape of the story that creates a through-arc even as we move into and out of those minds. In a beautiful symmetry this structural aspect of the novel mirrors the thematics of the crux points because cruxes surface moments of connection and disconnection. Peaks are often described as moments of connection, when everything holds together, while valleys surface separation, when there is no attachment.

Middle reading helps us reimagine the relationship between characters in a spatial way and understand that a "hero's journey" may be collective. The quest nature of this particular narrative connects two very different goals – the completion of a painting and the trip to the lighthouse – in such a way that a single high and low sentiment arc can pertain to both. Sentiment arc therefore offers us another way to think about this tension between the one and the many, especially for modernist novels that represent so many minds. In cases like Woolf's, the many and the one may not be in as clear tension, since the many are unified by one sentiment arc. These computational tools, then, can help us understand the unique ways that authors can create distributed heroines that nonetheless have strong, networked qualities, qualities that knit together the many and the one.

This interesting finding – that the sentiment arc can unify the experience of "the many" – dovetails with other computational methods that demonstrate that "the many" may not be quite as many as we assume. In *Enumerations* Andrew Piper suggests that very often actual linguistic descriptions of characters are quite similar. "There appears to be a strong degree of uniformity that exists between characters from different novels, even main characters, just as there seems to be a strong degree of uniformity between characters within the same novel. I have even found that characters tend to look more similar over the course of a novel than other types of nominal things" (2018). Piper's approach, coupled with sentiment analysis, offers us new ways to see how characters function outside the usual sense of Western individualism. We can see, for example, a similar linguistic phenomenon in the kinds of thematic resonances that occur in many of Woolf's cruxes. Even as she dips into individual minds, emotional peaks often occur when experiences are similar or shared.

Orlando offers yet another, albeit different, way of visualizing distributed heroines. Critical acclaim heralds the novel as experimental, and in many ways it is. In the case of the eponymous hero/ine, Orlando, we have a distributed character who is distributed both over time, since the character lives hundreds of years, and over traditional boundaries of character, since they wake up at one point as a woman. One might say that the "many" in Orlando is not the typical cast of characters, but the protagonist who experiences fluidity and multiplicity over time.

And yet this form of distributed character, which stretches the narrative in interesting ways, is also unified by a very clear sentiment arc. This is in no way to dismiss the innovative and experimental nature of the novel, but rather to help us see that Woolf experiments in different ways in each of her novels, and in each case what remains less experimental and more experimental changes. Sentiment arc gives us one way to be more precise about what is happening.

Figure 18 shows the sentiment arc of *Orlando*, in this case using a mean of seven different models since a multi-model comparison suggests widespread agreement. The clear sentiment arc takes a downward plunge earlier in the narrative than in *To the Lighthouse*, with the sawtooth pattern appearing after the dip. In spite of the sawtooth pattern later in the narrative, moreover, the various models generally agree. Finally, while the initial part of the novel evinces a deep plunge, afterward it is quite positive with a slightly noisy "heartbeat" pattern. Let's look at the key valley near the beginning of the narrative, for which models comport well. First Orlando waits for his lover Sasha in vain as the clock strikes twelve. Then the Thames freezes and thaws, causing widespread destruction. Finally Orlando, in "deep disgrace with the most powerful nobles of his time," retires to live in solitude.

It quickly becomes clear why this passage is graphed as an extreme low point. The chaos and destruction of the "disastrous winter which saw the frost, the flood, the deaths of many thousands" is coupled with Orlando's own emotional nadir. While Orlando's own pain is represented, therefore, as his isolated experience, it is followed by this mirror event of widespread destruction. Here we have a different kind of distributed heroine in which the negative emotional experience of Orlando is extended outward and shared by the many. In this case one might even say that the physical destruction of the many puts the individual heartbreak in perspective.

At least two elements of Woolf's storytelling are worth highlighting: Woolf creates an arc that is distributed to minor and even unnamed characters, even as this novel focuses on the hero of the title. Moreover, low points graph isolation, solitude, and dispersal even as these experiences are shared by many. So what are the high points?

The two peaks with the strongest confidence level are the conferring of the Most Noble Order of the Bath and Orlando's meeting with Mr. Pope. The readerly response may differ slightly from the sentiment arc, which fails to register the exaggeration and irony of these scenes. A similar question arises with the valley: are we really to conflate Orlando's disappointment in love with the physical catastrophe that befalls the collective? The sentiment arc cannot answer this, but it can show us that these events combine to create a single valley.

Once again the question becomes, how might this sentiment arc offer us something that would be useful for a reader? While one of Woolf's most experimental novels in terms of character and temporal expansion, *Orlando* offers through its sentiment arc a more unified and even, perhaps, traditional aspect of narrative to counterbalance the experimentation. Thematically, the

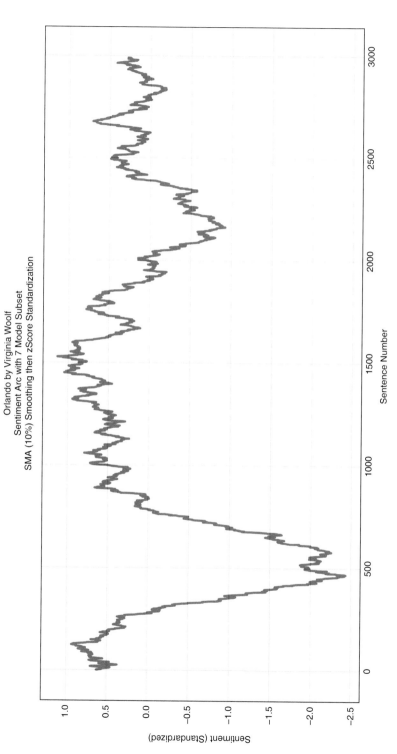

Figure 18 Mean of seven-model ensemble of Woolf's *Orlando*

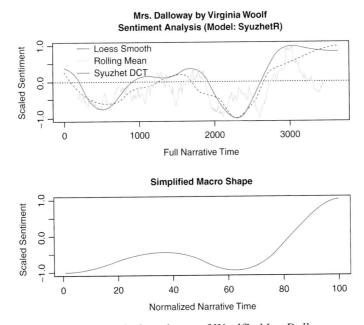

Figure 19 Smoothed sentiment of Woolf's *Mrs. Dalloway*

cruxes conform to both communal and individual understandings of tragedy (natural disaster, heartbreak) and the peaks conform to communal and individual understandings of success (awards, authorship/friendship).

In the case of *Orlando* sentiment analysis can offer the insight that a narrative can be experimental in certain ways while maintaining other elements that look far more like what has come before, even as they may be ironized. In fact, this reading of the novel is in keeping with one of the thematic currents of the novel: the past continues to live on in the present even as that present appears transformed.

2.6 Some Novels Are Harder to Plot

While the Woolf examples offer great ways of leveraging the strengths of sentiment analysis, they also show, quite rightly, that novels like Woolf's sometimes stretch the capacities of existing methods. Do some of Woolf's novels evince less structure? Existing methods of sentiment analysis suggest this to be the case. In our early research we relied on comportment between the various smoothing methods as a rough indicator of the difficulty of extracting a strong signal. If you're working with a single model, you can see evidence of this difficulty when the various methods of smoothing don't comport well. As a perfect example, Figure 19 shows our first attempt to graph *Mrs. Dalloway*.

Notice how the smoothed arcs place the narrative below neutral for much of the novel, whereas the Rolling Mean in gray exhibits more of a heartbeat pattern with numerous positive peaks. The sole point of near agreement falls shortly after sentence 2000. *Orlando* offers a much stronger signal. We can see that another of Woolf's more experimental novels, *The Waves*, also poses challenges to an ensemble approach, shown in Figure 20, though the mean does surface an overall wavelike pattern appropriately enough. At least with existing models, the conclusion is clear: some novels are harder to plot.

Unlike *The Waves*, however, a multi-model approach to *Mrs. Dalloway* offers more confidence and suggests that there may be a middle ground somewhere between the different smoothings we saw with the single arc. For the most part, many of these quite different models agree, as can be seen in Figure 21, though there is some noise. Can the newest AI transformer models add further confidence to our model? It would seem not. In fact, there is a lack of intra-model agreement among transformer models for *Mrs. Dalloway*, as you can see in Figure 22.

Here, then, we opt for a clustered close reading of an ensemble with some agreement. Most models surface cruxes that comport – for example, valleys surrounding Septimus Smith's mental breakdown and peaks like the one in which Mrs. Dalloway moves through her party "like a mermaid." But these clusters are more widely spaced, with a thirty-sentence spread characterizing the smaller clusters and a fifty-sentence spread more typical.

The deepest valley upon which the models comport is Clarissa's musings about all the terrible things that love and religion have inspired people to do: "Love and religion! thought Clarissa, going back into the drawing-room, tingling all over. How detestable, how detestable they are!" Another occurs when Septimus Smith thinks to himself that Shakespeare and Dante really hated humanity. Smaller peaks are, for the most part, somewhat muted in nature, like Lady Bruton musing on the threads that connect people in friendship. *Mrs. Dalloway* indicates a focus on "the one" with its title of a single character. But Woolf continues to experiment with the distributed heroine since crux points surface different characters' affective experiences including not just Septimus Smith and Mrs. Dalloway, but also Lady Bruton and Peter Walsh. Clarissa's reflections on the falsity of the unified self are mirrored in a sentiment arc that surfaces the distributed heroine of *To the Lighthouse*, but with a less strong and unified arc.

A visual EDA confirms the sense that this sentiment arc is much noisier and less integrative than that of *To the Lighthouse*. The aftershock of the war and Septimus Smith's breakdown seems to cause a breakdown in a strong sentiment arc as well. Still this sentiment arc surfaces continual ups and

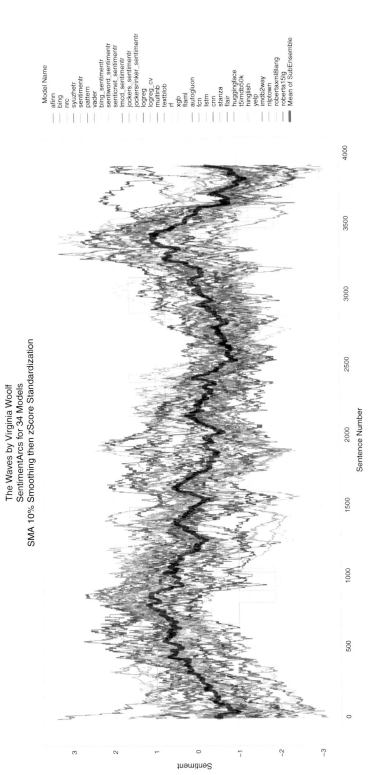

Figure 20 Ensemble of thirty-four smoothed models of Woolf's *The Waves*

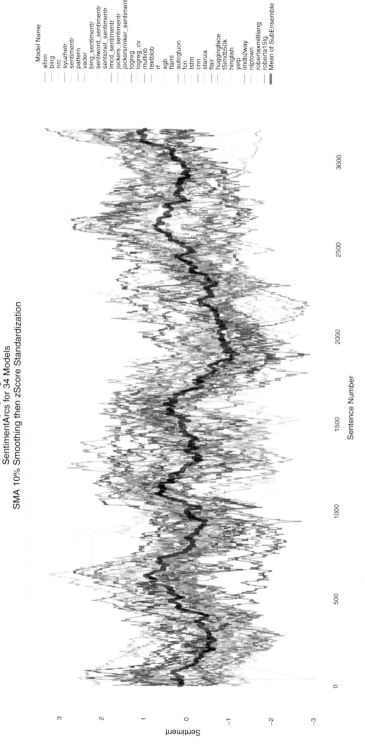

Figure 21 Ensemble of thirty-four smoothed models of Woolf's *Mrs. Dalloway*

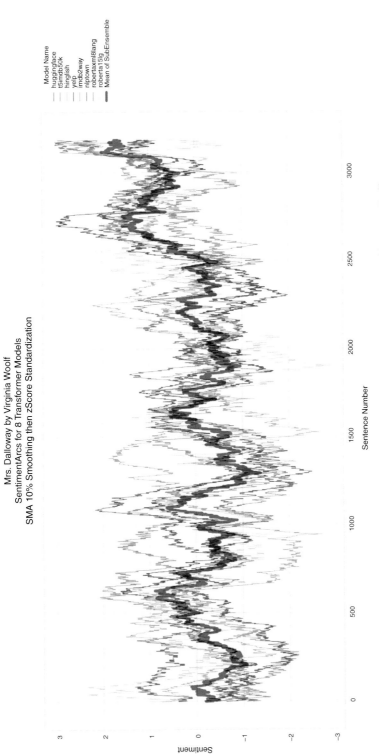

Figure 22 Ensemble of eight smoothed transformer models of Woolf's *Mrs. Dalloway*

downs in somewhat of a wavelike fashion. Although noisy, this may lend the novel the kind of sentiment fluctuation that gives us a pattern found in other narratives, even as it stretches the sentiment arc and challenges our current tools. Moreover, and in spite of the tragedy of Septimus Smith, *Mrs. Dalloway* actually exhibits a high peak near the end. The arc does remind us that a story can capture such negative sentiment while nonetheless creating a sloping, upward rise that ends on a neutral or perhaps even a slightly positive note.

2.7 Comparative Arcs

Scholars who have used sentiment analysis often compare the simplest shapes of the stories. But as we have seen, those highly smoothed shapes rarely capture much information about a particular narrative. Comparative approaches are possible, but they are best done using a finer-grained approach that takes into account elements described in the previous section like the noisiness of an arc, the more singular "fingerprint" pattern, and thematics surfaced by clustered close reading.

In these method case studies graphing the sentiment arcs of Woolf's oeuvre can afford us a comparative approach toward understanding the many different ways in which she experiments and pushes the boundaries of narrative. Both *To the Lighthouse* with its reference to the war in the short middle section and *Mrs. Dalloway* with the punctuated narrative of postwar trauma nonetheless offer certain elements of positive sentiment arc in peaks and a rising ending. In some ways, *To the Lighthouse* is the more positive sentiment arc. There are many moments of beauty and connection that create an upward pull. At the end of the novel, moreover, the quest is accomplished. Lily finishes her painting. The Ramsays make the trip to the lighthouse. And yet, viewed from the perspective of the most central, defining tragic line, one could view the most pronounced trend in the novel as one of downward trajectory. This complexity is mirrored on the thematic level of the narrative. Mrs. Ramsay is greatly attuned to the beauty and connection in the world but, beneath it all, she can't help but wonder if it is enough to counter the tragedy of the world. On the surface she is the optimist, but underneath she holds a tragic view of the world. We see these same dichotomies in the sentiment arc.

Mrs. Dalloway offers us a quite different but equally nuanced narrative. On the granular level it is far more negative than *To the Lighthouse*, with more valleys. But from a distance it is far more balanced, with waves in which troughs are paired with crests. We might conclude, then, that Woolf experiments with different ways to bring complexity to her novels, and much of the experiment often entails balancing opposites. Sentiment analysis, by offering us more ways to see the very different solutions Woolf writes into each novel, helps us understand her astonishing craft and the ways in which she does far more than just experiment with plot or a representation of interiority.

Mrs. Dalloway stands out in two important ways. On one hand, it's a "noisier" sentiment arc – more difficult to graph and smooth across the various models. It's not hard to argue that she is more experimental here than in *To the Lighthouse*, at least in this particular way. On the other hand, even as we see increasing "noise" in the sentiment arc of both *Mrs. Dalloway* and *The Waves*, we also see her engage with the more typical "bestseller" heartbeat pattern that I will examine in more detail later. It would be tempting to see Woolf's trajectory as increasingly pessimistic, especially given our knowledge that she finally lost her struggle with depression. But comparative arcs reveal a more complex sense of the sentiment that shapes her writing.

2.8 The Sense of an Ending

Ever since Frank Kermode's *The Sense of an Ending* we've understood the importance of endings for interpreting narrative. In both *Mrs. Dalloway* and *To the Lighthouse* there is a positive emotional peak near the end. But what of the end itself? The DCT in particular fluctuates enormously and the more smoothed versions should be evaluated with higher levels of skepticism. The simple moving average, which we favor as a better approach for human-in-the-loop validation, performs better, but we still encounter flaring of our ensemble method at both beginnings and ends. This suggests less coherence and less signal, and clustered close reading is less likely to be helpful. There is a simple reason for all these difficulties: when the window contains less than its typical 10 percent of data, this method of extracting signal performs less well.

This current weakness of the model is an active area of research both in our lab and elsewhere. Currently we favor using a shrinking window, available with the SentimentArcs, but Jon Chun hopes to have even more sophisticated methods available soon. At present, however, sentiment analysis is a middle reading approach in the literal sense that it helps us explore the middle of narrative, but it sometimes offers less signal as to the end points.

With ensemble models that exhibit significant flaring near the endpoints, as in *To the Lighthouse*, the sense of an ending must rely entirely on the reader and close analysis. However, in cases where the ensemble surfaces general agreement, as it does for *Great Expectations*, we can still ascertain a sense of the ending. Notice how much the models in Figure 23 flare for the beginning but comport fairly well (with only a single outlier) to model a positive rise for the

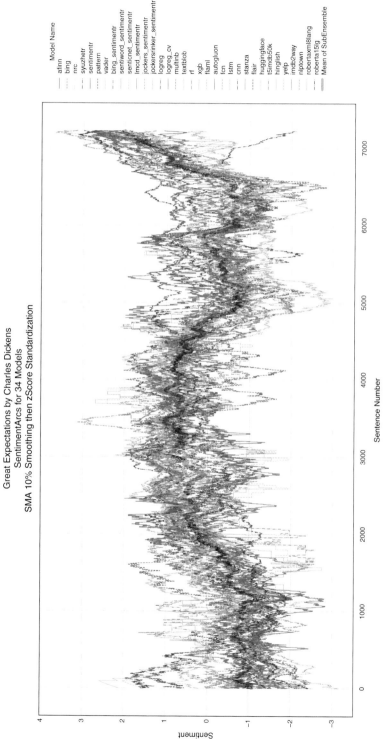

Figure 23 Ensemble of thirty-four smoothed models of Dickens's *Great Expectations*

ending. Of course, as we have already seen, models sometimes disagree in the same way that human analysis does. A good case in point is Henry James's *Portrait of a Lady*. Scholars disagree as to the valence of the ending, and an ensemble, shown in Figure 24, suggests fairly significant disagreement as well. If we explore the mean, we can see that the vast majority of models graph the end point as below neutral. While there are peaks and valleys, the general sense of the narrative is a movement downward as a tragic decline. But there are a significant number of outliers that comport with a more positive reading of the ending, both because there is a final upward movement and because the models end higher than the lowest valleys. Simply put, the ensemble reflects the same disagreement we see in scholarly analysis.

We have one more method of trying to get a sense of an ending. We can explore the final crux and then use human judgment to determine if the narrative that follows is more positive in valence (indicating a rise) or continues in the same or even the more negative direction seen in Figure 25. The last scene modeled occurs when Isabel Archer meets with Goodwood, whom she refuses: we can validate that it is indeed negative. How does the narrative proceed, from a readerly perspective, after this final crux? There is no reversal or choice in which Isabel Archer is liberated from her unhappy marriage. The lack of a clear reversal would suggest a tragic ending. And yet we do have a small glimmer of hope since she affirms her independence as she travels alone to Rome. Will she find some happiness in her independence? The answer is not clear, and the models reflect this. Even more so than in *To the Lighthouse*, however, the overall tragic nature of the narrative can be seen in the very long downward slope. There is an ambiguity in the sense of the ending, but the general sense of the narrative is undoubtedly tragic.

One can contrast this general tragic shape with another novel that is equally challenging to graph: George Eliot's *Middlemarch*, seen in Figure 26. *Middlemarch* is also quite a long novel, so caution is warranted since the excluded end is longer than it would be in the case of shorter narratives. In the case of *Middlemarch* and *Portrait of a Lady*, the sentiment arcs are surprisingly similar. Both novels evince a fairly steady downward arc even as there are some peaks or plateaus in the middle. While the entire narrative evinces a downward tragic plunge, however, there is enough of a rise near the end of *Middlemarch* to give a sense of optimism. Like *Great Expectations*, we have a much longer movement upward near the end. Moreover, models are split evenly as to whether the end of the narrative is located above or below neutral.

Perhaps a more interesting question is whether modernist novels like *Portrait of a Lady* often exhibit these tragic declines and whether Eliot has written a sentiment arc that, barring its final upward trend, would become popular

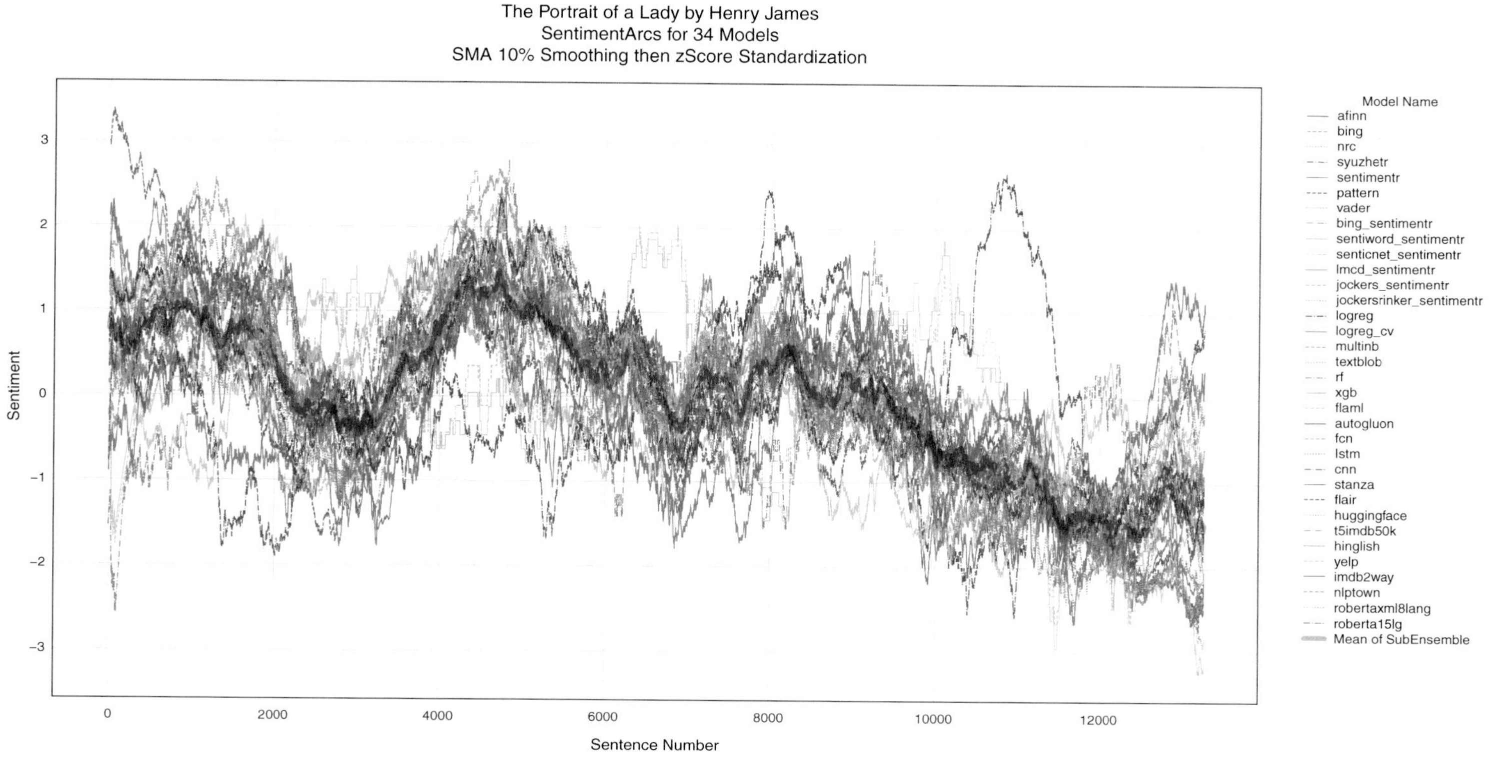

Figure 24 Ensemble of thirty-four smoothed models of James's *The Portrait of a Lady*

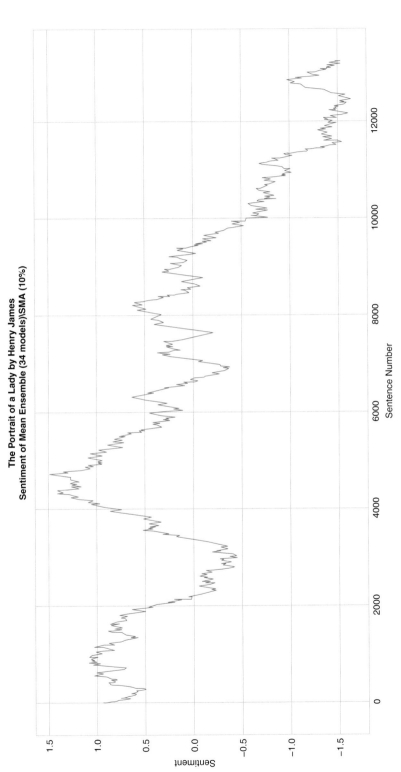

Figure 25 Mean of thirty-four model ensemble of James's *The Portrait of a Lady*

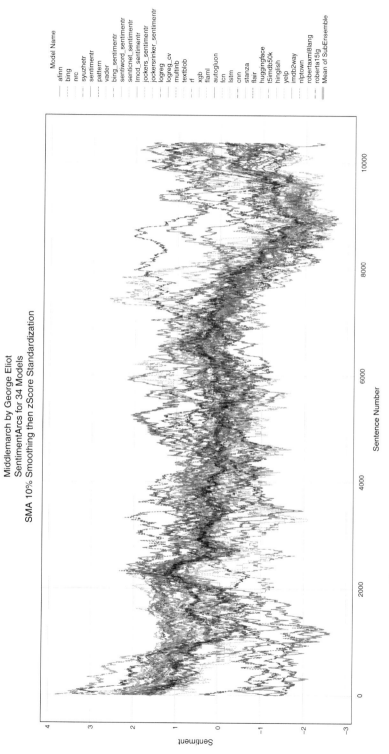

Middlemarch by George Eliot
SentimentArcs for 34 Models
SMA 10% Smoothing then zScore Standardization

Model Name
afinn
bing
nrc
syuzhetr
sentimentr
pattern
vader
bing_sentimentr
sentiword_sentimentr
senticnet_sentimentr
lmcd_sentimentr
jockers_sentimentr
jockersrinker_sentimentr
logreg
logreg_cv
multinb
textblob
rf
xgb
flaml
autogluon
fcn
lstm
cnn
stanza
flair
huggingface
t5imdb50k
hinglish
yelp
imdb2way
nlptown
robertaxml8lang
roberta15lg
Mean of SubEnsemble

Sentiment

Figure 26 Ensemble of thirty-four smoothed models of Eliot's *Middlemarch*

with the modernists. I can attest that this shape is rather unusual, and the similarity of sentiment arcs is surprising. Scholar David Kramer asks whether George Eliot is really a proto-modernist, and his argument focuses on the shift from plot to dialogue and thought. Sentiment arc offers additional ways of considering the question. Of course this limited case study opens onto questions of "representativeness" that Andrew Piper (2020) so eloquently formulates. Are these shapes more frequent in modernist novels than in novels written before or after? One would need to graph a larger corpus of novels to generalize. Moreover, as we saw with Woolf, not all modernists employ this particular narrative shape, but it's an interesting question to ask whether different periods favor different shapes of stories. It's also worth considering that these novels are harder to graph than many more traditional ones.

The more novels we graph, the more we can identify just what constitutes an unusual shape and what percentage of narratives are difficult to model. In this sense, therefore, our middle reading prepares us to ask some distant reading questions even as the distant reading of simple shapes has led us to ask questions more suited to close and middle reading. To really answer how unusual *Middlemarch* is, we need a better sense of what is typical. I turn now to a closer examination of more typical curves before a deeper dive into the many, varied shapes of stories.

3 The Shapes of Stories

In *The Bestseller Code* Archer and Jockers describe "bestseller curves": sentiment arcs that resemble a heartbeat. Let's see if bestseller curves apply to "early" bestsellers like *Robinson Crusoe*, shown in Figure 27 using a single model for a first pass. With a single model, this one does. Models vary slightly when examining the more complex ensemble shown in Figure 28, but all exhibit this undulation in waves, with the transformer model, RoBERTa, offering four dips instead of three. The mean offers us three peaks and three valleys that are well spaced and that resemble bestseller curves. The second shipwreck of the tale forms the deepest valley of the text, after which the graph's dips are less extreme and the narrative curves gently rise.

Dips after the shipwreck focus on perceived fear of conflict (valley #2) when Crusoe discovers there are others on the island and on the arrival of a ship and scenes of violence (valley #3). Clustered close reading of peaks surface religious aspects of the narrative as Crusoe reads the Bible and is thankful that God has provided for him (#2) and then teaches Friday about God (#3). Solitude and companionship with Friday (peaks) offer a form of happiness that is in contrast

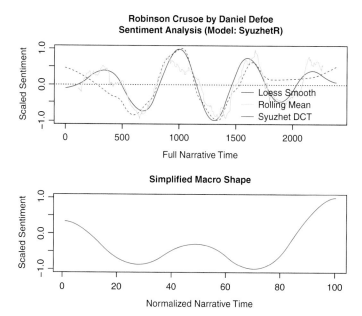

Figure 27 Smoothed sentiment of Defoe's *Robinson Crusoe*

to the events (valleys) that occur with "the many," thus setting the stage for a novel that highlights individualism.

Contemporary secular readers may be less apt to see the reading of the Bible or the missionary aspects of peak #3 with the same valence as earlier readers. And yet this approach still helps surface cruxes that may have resonated with readers at the time. Even more astonishing is that a book that was a bestseller in its day, with six printings in four months, exhibits the same kinds of curves as a contemporary blockbuster.

Episodic ups and downs produce fairly uniform wavelike patterns of positive and negative language on either side of the x-axis. Are these curves present in earlier forms of episodic narrative – for example, the *Odyssey*, shown in Figure 29? Indeed the *Odyssey* evinces curves with a slight descending slope and a final upward trajectory when Odysseus achieves his quest to return home. In the case of *Robinson Crusoe* the initial deep valley is followed by a series of curves that ascend as Crusoe discovers that he is able to provide for himself and find connection to both God and his friend, Friday. In the case of the *Odyssey* there is a gradual descent as Odysseus's attempt to return home is thwarted time and time again. Depending on the story, "bestseller" curves may gradually ascend, fluctuate evenly above and below the x-axis, or gradually descend.

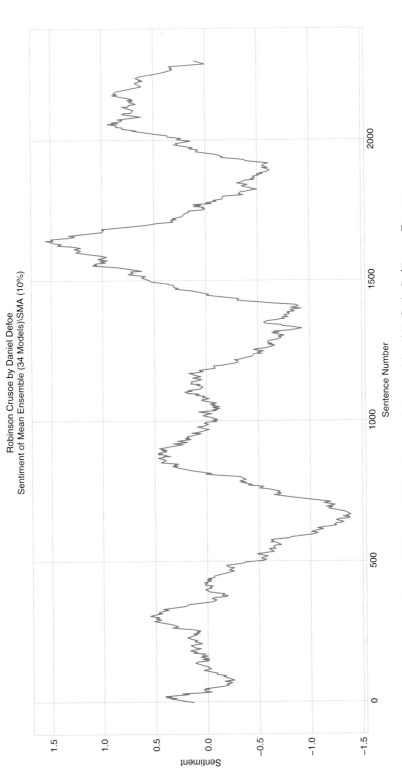

Figure 28 Mean of thirty-four-model ensemble of Defoe's *Robinson Crusoe*

Figure 29 SMA versus LOWESS smoothed sentiment of Homer's *Odyssey* (translated by Wilson)

Can curves like these help surface a general property of many narratives shared across time periods, thereby earning the more apt moniker "storyteller curves"? Figure 30 shows the sentiment arc of the classic American novel *The Great Gatsby*, surfaced using the mean since models comport well. In *The Great Gatsby* both the height and width of curves vary, but we have the typical emotional pattern of undulating peaks and valleys. Like *The Waves* and *Mrs. Dalloway*, this pattern – what I term "storyteller curves" since it appears in more than just contemporary bestsellers – is a curve that takes many forms. This differs from the narratives we examined earlier like *To the Lighthouse*, *Portrait of a Lady*, and *Howards End*, which seem to have fewer peaks and valleys. We call this new shape storyteller curves, then, as a way to emphasize multiple, repeated peaks and valleys as opposed to narratives that, as in *To the Lighthouse*, surface a simpler shape.

We have surfaced it not just in novels but also in plays and screenplays, speeches and *Shark Tank* pitches. It's not necessarily indicative of plot, although we have found that storyteller curves almost always surface latent properties of plot when they exist. Storyteller curves suggest an emotional "roller coaster ride" that unfolds over time as the language of sentiment ranges high and then low in repeated fashion. One could imagine that shaping an emotional experience of this nature is a fundamental skill of any good storyteller, although it could equally be an emergent property of good storytelling.

3.1 Storyteller Curves

There are also ways that narratives can combine a simple shape with storyteller curves. A good example is Dickens's *Great Expectations*, shown again here in Figure 31. From a distance what stands out is the way in which the narrative evinces one giant wave structure. It seems closer to Freytag's pyramid, only with a final rising ending. If we ignore the ending and focus only on this dominant shape, I would call this a "person-on-a-hill" structure, a sentiment arc that, with the exception of the ending, suggests a rags-to-riches-to-rags model, also known as an Icarus story.

Clustered close reading allows us to surface fairly strong agreement across multiple models. The lowest valley right before the main "hill" shape surfaces the moment the protagonist, young Pip, encounters a stranger in a pub and is given some money, foreshadowing the gift of his anonymous patron soon to come. On the other side of the hill, the sentiment arc surfaces the reappearance of a stranger, this time on Pip's stairs in London after he has made his rags-to-riches journey. Pip has learned that his anonymous patron is not the wealthy Miss Havisham, as he had hoped, but the escaped convict Magwitch, whom he

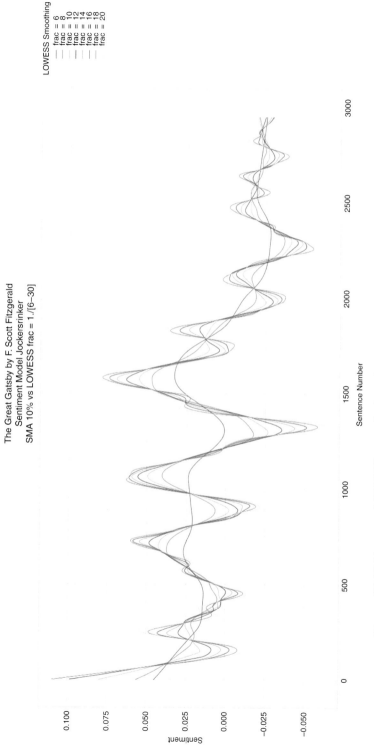

Figure 30 SMA versus LOWESS smoothed sentiment of F. Scott Fitzgerald's *The Great Gatsby*

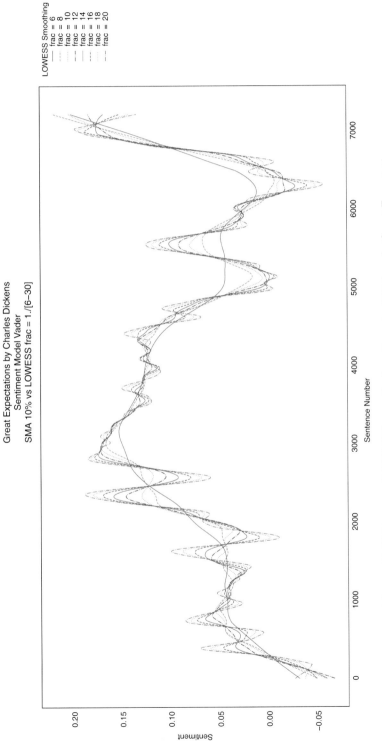

Figure 31 SMA versus LOWESS smoothed sentiment of Dickens's *Great Expectations*

helped long ago. The riches he experienced in London had not been all he had hoped, and the "Icarus" story is followed by two more dips, the first during the fire at Miss Havisham's due to which Pip is injured and the second during Pip's departure by boat to bring Magwitch to safety.

Note there is a very strong reversal right before the end of the novel that can give us a sense of the ending, especially since we confirmed earlier (Figure 24) that most models comport well. A modern reader might be surprised by the final peak, during which Magwitch is condemned to death. One might not expect one of the highest emotional points of the novel to fall on such a moment. It makes more sense, however, when the story is read as a redemption narrative: Magwitch feels his death is justified and he and Pip solidify a moment of connection. Dickens himself experienced uncertainty over how to conclude and he was persuaded by his friend, the novelist Edward Bulwer-Lytton, to add a happy ending in which Pip is inferred to marry Estella. The sentiment arc tells a different story, however, surfacing a final peak in the redemption moment rather than in the section implying a happy ending.

A granular approach, however, complicates this simple shape, for you'll notice in Figure 31 that there is a constant undulating smaller set of wave shapes even as the larger single wave rises and falls. The LOWESS smoothing method gives us a good sense of what I call this curves-on-a-hill shape. Perhaps the use of much smaller storyteller curves keeps the sentiment arc rising and falling even as there is a simpler shape. These ups and downs on the hill are somewhat noisier. Different smoothings locate the peaks across a wider spread than elsewhere, and you can see this in the LOWESS smoothings: a slight change in the smoothing window can easily mean the difference between a peak and valley. This "noisiness," as we've seen, is often accompanied by emotional ambivalence. True to previous examples, clustered close reading surfaces moments in *Great Expectations* that already contain the shadow of the inevitable downward arc even as they surface at the top of small hills and near the crest of the larger one. In one crux, Pip arrives at Mr Jaggers and the cab driver mentions that he's afraid of Mr Jaggers. Another clustered peak surfaces the extravagant and lavish lifestyle Pip is able to lead, which causes his friend Herbert great anxiety due to his limited resources.

We can also see smaller storyteller curves in other simple shapes like Joseph Conrad's *Heart of Darkness* in Figure 32. The more distant shape of the narrative evinces a "person-in-a-hole" shape. The opening peak, which is quite high, centers on Marlow's fascination with the snake of the river on the map, which enchants him and leads him on his journey to Africa. Several models also locate a second peak right before the steamer is fixed and the

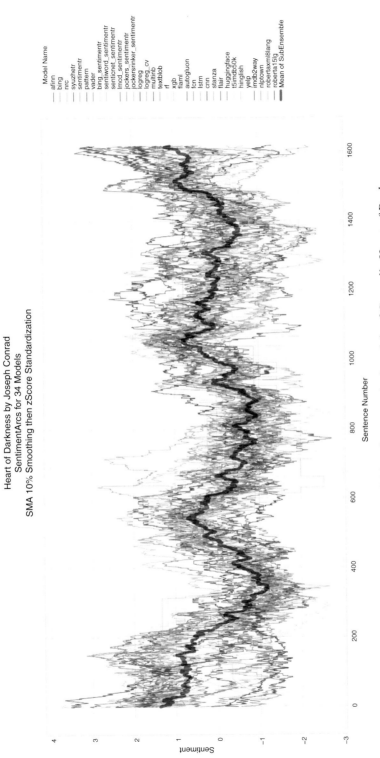

Figure 32 Ensemble of thirty-four smoothed models of Conrad's *Heart of Darkness*

journey downriver begins. This second peak surfaces a sublime sense of the natural world that would seem to mirror Marlow's fascination with the map:

> Beyond the fence the forest stood up spectrally in the moonlight, and through the dim stir, through the faint sounds of that lamentable courtyard, the silence of the land went home to one's very heart, – its mystery, its greatness, the amazing reality of its concealed life.

A bit later in this section, which is part of the final peak before the descent, the narrative continues:

> The smell of mud, of primeval mud, by Jove! was in my nostrils, the high stillness of primeval forest was before my eyes; there were shiny patches on the black creek. The moon had spread over everything a thin layer of silver – over the rank grass, over the mud, upon the wall of matted vegetation standing higher than the wall of a temple, over the great river could see through a somber gap glittering, glittering, as it flowed broadly by without a murmur. All this was great, expectant, mute.

Different models rank this peak at different heights. Unsurprisingly, there is some ambivalence, which is typical of the sublime. Marlowe wonders "whether the stillness on the face of the immensity looking at us two were meant as an appeal or as a menace." The sentiment of the scene is difficult for Marlow himself to interpret.

Divergence in intensity of the final peak, which lies on the other side of the journey, offers further room for analysis. Clustered close reading yields fair confidence in the location, when Marlow visits the intended of Kurtz after his return home. The majority of models graph the moment as quite high, confirming the final rise that constitutes the simpler hole shape. On one hand, it's hard to argue with the notion that the intended, however deluded, offers a beautifully humane and touching tribute to Kurtz. On the other hand, her understanding of Kurtz is clearly limited since Marlow decides not to tell her of his final words, "the horror, the horror." Her love, in other words, is sustained by a lie.

During the midsection of the narrative, the journey is graphed for the most part below neutral, and Conrad makes use of muted storyteller curves even as there is a larger trend toward a hole-like shape. How does Conrad create emotional peaks during this journey, which remains negatively valenced? Clustered close reading yields a number of peaks that comport fairly well: a description of Kurtz as a prodigy, the moment Marlow exclaims that "We shall have rivets!" to fix the steamer, and key moments of reprieve when those on the boat discover the woodpile and then repel an attack with the steam whistle.

Clustered valleys include the description of the Swede's suicide, the chaos of the station, and the "very grave situation" with Kurtz's illness. We also find valleys as those on the boat worry about an attack, are then attacked, and learn about Kurtz's obsessive hunt for ivory. The valleys near the end of the hole occur in scenes with Kurt, during his illness and while describing "the horror, the horror."

Chinua Achebe critiqued the extent of the novel's dehumanization of Africans, and the sentiment arc raises further questions about how we might view Conrad's own implication in the colonialist and imperialist project he describes. While the sentiment arc does not offer a definitive answer, it does offer points of reference. High points for the most part center on the natural world or on the hopes and dreams of characters – whether Marlowe's or Kurtz's intended's – that are countered by the larger narrative. Moreover, key valleys are surfaced when describing whites in negative ways, including both at the station and in the meeting with the Russian.

On the other hand, readers are right to object to a story that evinces a person-in-the-hole shape for a journey to Africa. Many of the valleys surfaced, moreover, depict this dehumanization of Africans, thereby confirming that it is not just a minor element of the novel but appears at key crux points. For this reason one can conclude that the problematic representation of Africans helps form the very shape of the story. Exploring sentiment arc may help us further understand ways in which Conrad's own biases lie implicit in his storyteller curves.

Finally, just how implicated these computational models are in racist and colonialist linguistic use is a pressing area of research.[20] Because word embeddings and transformer models rely on contextual use patterns, they can easily replicate existing biases in their evaluation of language. Ultimately the approach should never replace our critical reading and all the context and knowledge – including our human values that rightly condemn dehumanization – that we bring to our reading experience.

3.2 Tragic Curves

An advantage of the simpler models for sentiment analysis is the white-box capability to assess how well a dictionary captures the language of the text. Sometimes, however, simpler models don't work well. Known for its complexity, Toni Morrison's *Beloved* is one such example. With lexical models valleys illuminate moments of conflict, as we might expect, but the positive moments are harder to make sense of. None of the cruxes comport with readerly analysis and some seem downright wrong. For example, one of the highest emotional

---

[20] See work published out of DAIR.AI by Elvis and out of IBM Watson by Sean Sodha.

peaks in the novel occurs when Sethe kills her baby in response to the arrival of the schoolteacher, who has come to take them back into slavery. How could this possibly be?

A close analysis of the scene right before that moment yields a bit more insight into how the model could err. As Sethe climbs into the cart to be taken away after the killing, her profile is described "against a cheery blue sky," striking to the onlookers "with its clarity." Sethe's behavior is contrasted with the judgment of the Black folks watching: "Was her head a bit too high? Her back a little too straight?" A simple lexical reading could easily mistake this scene description as more positive than it is. Directly following is also a contrary-to-fact description of what might have happened had Sethe not been so assured in her moral clarity. The community would have begun singing and the sound "would have quickly wrapped around her, like arms to hold and steady her on the way." Linguistically, we can see how challenging this scene is to parse from a computational standpoint.

The narrative arc is further complicated because story time is quite different from discursive time. The narrative is punctuated by flashbacks that give us the backstory of Sethe's escape from slavery as well as the Sweet Home group's preparation for their flight to freedom. There are also many different stories interwoven. Paul D, Stamp Paid, Denver, and Beloved recount histories, giving us an extreme version of a distributed heroine where the cruxes dip into different characters *and* different time periods. What happens when past events intrude on the present in so pressing a manner? With such complexity, is there still an underlying narrative shape?

A comparison of models suggests significant noise, seen in Figure 33. The inter-model agreement is poor, indicating a clustered close reading approach won't work well. And while there is some coherence in a simple lexical model, the findings don't comport well with readerly experience. Comparing the mean of the ensemble with that of just the transformers suggests that choosing a transformer might offer the best compromise in this situation since it follows the mean fairly closely and there is intra-model coherence. Compare an ensemble of transformers, Figure 34, with the mean of Figure 33. Moreover, several transformer models comport (Hugging Face and RoBERTa) and these two share broad similarities with other models like FLAIR and TextBlob, a similarity that inspires a bit more confidence. In this case RoBERTa seems to perform best when we look at the cruxes, as we do in a moment. This suggests that sometimes, especially with narratives that are challenging to graph, selecting an optimal model yields the best results.

Transformers evaluate that unusual peak around Sethe's murder quite differently from the simpler ones. In this midsection of the narrative, they surface

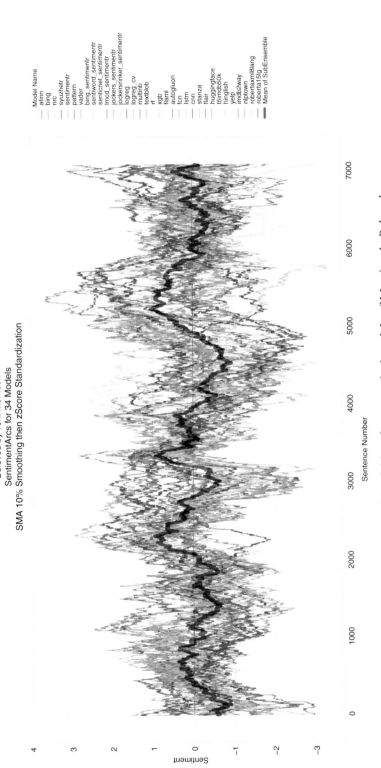

Figure 33 Ensemble of thirty-four smoothed models of Morrison's *Beloved*

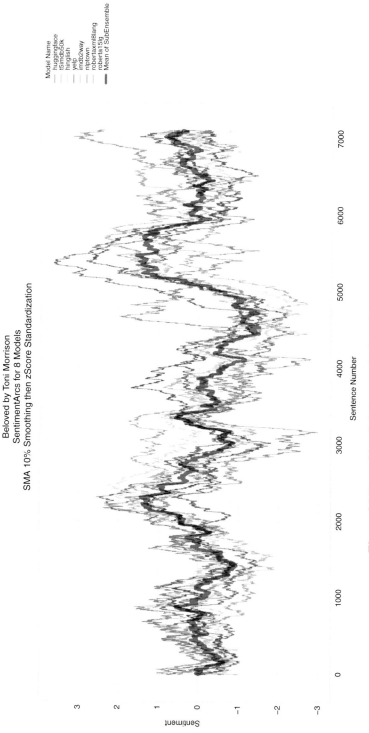

Figure 34 Ensemble of eight smoothed models of Morrison's *Beloved*

a descending sloped line – a tragic descent – in place of that high peak. While SentimentR surfaced a very large peak during the infanticide scene, RoBERTa surfaced a small peak, seen in Figure 35. This key scene during which Sethe kills her child still appears as a peak, but according to this model it is closer to neutral. Neutral peaks and valleys can signify moments that are emotionally ambivalent with conflicting sentiment that cancels out. This evaluation of the moment seems to make more sense. Even as Sethe feels pride that she has helped her child escape slavery through death, the reaction of the larger community reveals a more tragic understanding of events.

The larger difference between this transformer model and the simpler models is the replacement of more typical and highly peaked storyteller curves with what I call tragic curves. We've already seen curves-on-a-hill and curves-in-a-hole. Here we see a more general shape – in this case a descending line with smaller storyteller curves (or spikes here, because less smoothed) to propel the narrative forward. There is a downward descent into tragedy with small curves throughout.

This tragic descent resonates thematically with events in this midsection: hubris is clearly linked with tragic outcomes. Baby Suggs, in spite of her hesitation, celebrates the escape into freedom of several of her family members. The party, with its excess, results in community jealousy, which in turn leads to the failure of the community to warn the family when the slave catchers appear in town. Pride also distinguishes Sethe's reaction to her murder.

The peak just before these tragic curves takes place as a flashback, after Sethe's arrival at her mother-in-law's home. Baby Suggs cares for Sethe and helps her recover from her physical wounds, and there is still optimism that Halle, Sethe's husband, will arrive shortly. As the narrative continues, both we and Sethe learn that Halle will never arrive. Baby Suggs also gives up hope. Meanwhile, Beloved's behavior becomes more sinister. Readerly analysis comports with the shape of tragic curves that descend following the escape from slavery.

The large peak after the tragic curves is yet another flashback, only this time the memory recounts the preparations by the Sweet Home group as they plan for their escape. The peak moment occurs just before the description of events that bring adjustment after adjustment, the language a series of noes that recount the continual altering of plans to escape slavery.

While the first peak recounts an escape from freedom that will soon be followed by isolation from the community, this second peak focuses on a collective endeavor as the Sweet Home group works together toward a shared plan. This return to a collective sense of identity is mirrored in the reconnection of Sethe's family with the larger community in the final scenes.

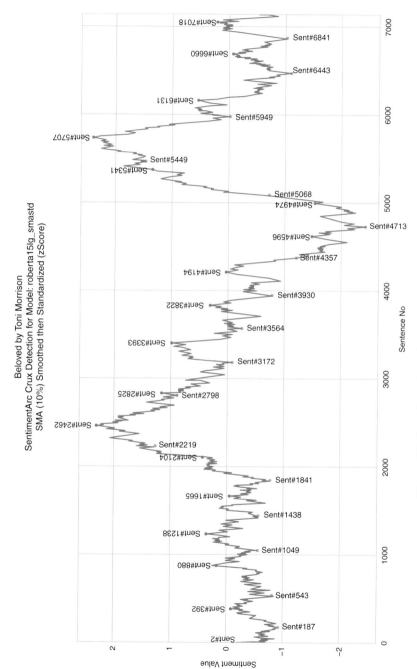

Figure 35 Crux detection of smoothed Morrison's *Beloved*

Before this second peak, at the absolute valley of the narrative – upon which all models agree – various characters remember their past and experience emotional grieving as they process their history. This valley, moreover, is a distributed heroine valley since it collects the voices of many, each unique and isolated in its pain and yet interwoven as voices united in a shared sentiment arc. This nadir comes right before the process of rebuilding the community that will happen with the rise out of tragedy.

Perhaps most striking is the way that a narrative that weaves back and forth in time surfaces two peaks that are flashbacks, while the valley represents moments in the present as the characters finally process the past. The other fully "present" part of the narrative occurs in the first part of the model. Here we see a noisier, spiked set of waves that hover around neutral.

This too makes sense from a narrative point of view. In spite of Paul D's return and some sentiment peaks – like the trip to a carnival – the beginning of the narrative mirrors the difficulty of experiencing deep sentiment, both positive and negative, because of the persistence of trauma. Perhaps this also explains why some of the peaks in the tragic curves involve sentiments that are unusual for a peak and more typical of a valley. In one tragic curved peak, for example, Denver encourages Beloved to cry.

Tragic curves lead finally to the process of grieving in the deepest valley. Paul D must come to terms with Sethe's actions and Sethe must come to terms with Halle's fate. Remembering – with the second peak of all that happened at Sweet Home before the escape – also makes possible the rise out of tragedy. There is, in Morrison's narrative, a peak that comes after tragedy, but it is hard won and comes only after great suffering, a conscious act of remembering the past, and the passage of time.

When Jon Chun and I began working with the latest transformer models our natural assumption was the newer AI models would work best. This was probably partially due to our work with GPT-2 and GPT-3 (Elkins and Chun, 2020), which revealed that, for language generation, transformer models far outperform simpler language models. In the case of Toni Morrison's *Beloved* this also proved to be the case for sentiment analysis. However, it's also the case that for the most part we have been disappointed that these more sophisticated models don't always outperform simpler ones. Surprisingly, state-of-the-art models can often struggle with common text as can be seen when different transformer models like BERT, RoBERTa, and T5 produce more disagreements than simpler lexical models like Syuzhet, Bing, and NRC (Chun 2021). Like a human foreign language learner, AI transformers rely on a more sophisticated level of interpretation that can sometimes be woefully wrong.

3.3 Ideal and Material Curves

It seems only fitting to employ a machine reading sentiment approach to a narrative that forefronts a machine that can both read and feel: Ian McEwan's novel *Machines Like Me*. McEwan's title is an ironic nod to the ambiguity in "me." Who are the real machines – the AI named Adam or his human foil, Charlie? That we can use a machine method of surfacing sentiment arc begs the question: is it the case that most human readers engage in predictable emotional responses to narrative as if they were machines themselves?

We should not be surprised that McEwan artfully employs storyteller curves since he is a perennial best-selling author. He also offers us one more way to interpret the sentiment arc. Instead of mapping cruxes to characters or plot points, the novel's curves often map ideas and (alternate) historical events as key inflection points. In this way both human dreams and human history – the ideal and the material – emerge in the same kind of distributed character pattern we've seen earlier. Comparison between the mean of many models and Jockers-Rinker suggests that this single model comports fairly well here. A quick cluster analysis confirms that in only one case did several of the other models perform better, locating a peak crux a bit earlier, at the end of chapter 8. We focus for the most part here, then, on the single model shown in Figure 36.

In the case of this novel, and quite unlike what we saw in *Orlando*, the sentiment arc highlights the extent to which the protagonist Charlie feels out of sync with the events that surround him: he is an "islet of hopes" during a valley that is an "ocean of national sorrow" (valley 1179). Similarly, although Charlie marches in labor union strikes (valley 2429), Charlie admits that he himself – in his financial speculations – makes nothing, constructs nothing, and thus feels somewhat disconnected from another event that forms a low point of the narrative. The emotional valleys of the novel often surface these larger material, historical circumstances, even as they are in contrast to Charlie's own emotional state. Other valleys highlight not history but the darker sides of idealism: a suicide following a rape, with an implication that the death might have been prevented had a friend not kept a secret (3423). The valley that surfaces the rapist's confession likewise shows us idealism's dark side: his desire to be loved.

Crux peaks surface idealism even as these ideals are imbued (for the reader) with uncertainty or uneasiness: Charlie's belief that his own consciousness makes him superior to the AI (1605), descriptions of the AI, Adam, who falls in love and writes haikus (3071), Alan Turing's solution to the mathematical problem P/NP, which unleashes technological progress for good and ill (3896), and the moment our protagonist is mistaken for a machine (4665):

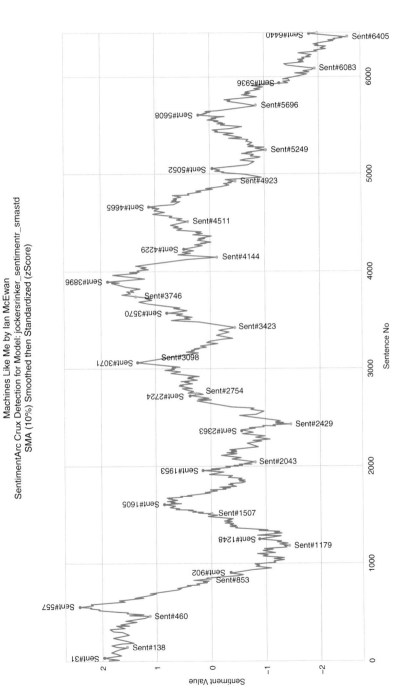

Figure 36 Crux detection of smoothed McEwan's *Machines Like Me*

a triumph for the AI, who convinces as human, but a less certain one for our human Charlie.

The dreams of artificial Adam (5608), which include the full extent of human emotion and reason, are also highlighted in these peaks, and they are counterbalanced by emotional valleys that include the worst of the human condition: valleys that surface global warming and unemployment, rape, and murder. The sentiment arc, in other words, reveals the conflict between the ideal and the material, the AI and the human, with all serving as distributed characters in the novel. Only near the end of the narrative do we see a valley crux in which Charlie's sentiment merges with the personal tragedy of the AI, Adam, alongside the tragedy of the world around them. A politician's assassination is coupled with the tragedy at home. This ending only furthers the sense that any human dream of creating artificial general intelligence is likely to be met with a tragic outcome shared by all.

3.4 Do Some Stories Lack Curves?

Do some successful stories lack curves? Here is a look at the first four volumes of *In Search of Lost Time* by Marcel Proust. One of the four volumes presented in Figures 37, 38, 39, and 40 often proves the most challenging for readers. Can you guess which one? If you guessed Figure 39 – *The Guermantes Way* – you would be right.

Proust is experimental with his sentence structure, and André Gide turned down the first volume – a decision he later came to regret – because of it. But this first novel, *Swann's Way* (Figure 37), is less experimental with its sentiment arc. Some have argued that this first volume is more typical of nineteenth-century narrative, and this claim is bolstered by these strong storyteller curves.

Two of the other narratives look a bit more like other shapes we've seen. *In the Shadow of Young Girls in Flower* (Figure 38) looks more like *Heart of Darkness*. *Sodom and Gomorrah* (Figure 40), by contrast, looks more like *Great Expectations* – a person-on-a-hill with some smaller curves to propel the story forward. *The Guermantes Way* exhibits some strong curves in the second half of the narrative that might remind you of Woolf's *To the Lighthouse* with its extreme peak and valley. In fact, however, the volume was actually conceived as two separate volumes, with the second half beginning at the midpoint of the graph you see. If the sentiment arc of the second part of the narrative seems like the arc of an entirely different novel, to some extent it is. Part Two of *The Guermantes Way* is a person-on-a-hill shape while Part One is flat, ending with a tragic decline.

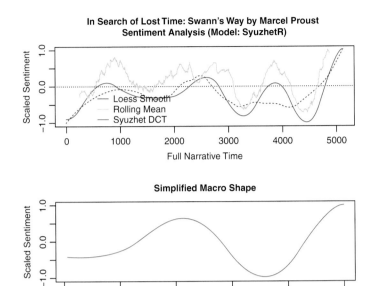

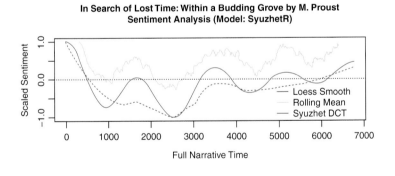

Figure 37 Smoothed sentiment of Proust's *Swann's Way*

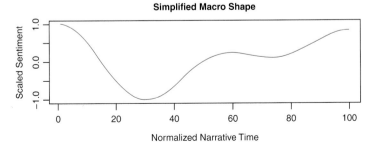

Figure 38 Smoothed sentiment of Proust's *Within a Budding Grove*

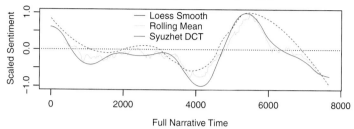

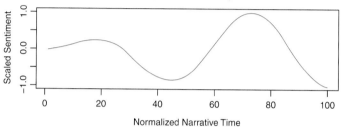

Figure 39 Smoothed sentiment of Proust's *The Guermantes Way*

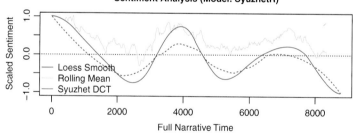

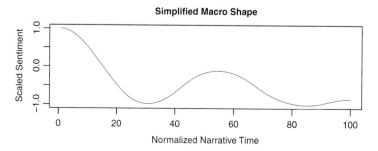

Figure 40 Smoothed sentiment of Proust's *Sodom and Gomorrah*

This beginning of *The Guermantes Way* is, quite simply, one of the longest flat sections I have encountered. This unusual pattern validates the curious readerly experience I've seen. I had always attributed this reaction to cultural differences since the volume describes an aristocratic world quite foreign to most. While there are undoubtedly many factors involved, the shape of the story confirms the sense that there is something different in this narrative structure. We see a definite flattening of the curves and the absence of the kind of sentiment peaks and valleys that give many stories their shape.

Ben Blatt (2017) has done some intriguing analysis of the ways in which novelists change their writing once they become successful. Proust won the prestigious Prix Goncourt award for *The Shadow of Young Girls* in 1919. *The Guermantes Way* was first published in two volumes in the years that followed, 1920 and 1921. If Proust demonstrates his craft of writing by using impossibly long sentences in all his novels, he may be experimenting with something even harder in this writing that follows the prize: writing a narrative without curves.[21] We might add a new shape to our collection, one I'll call "person-on-the-plain" in honor of Proust's alternate title of volume four: *Cities on the Plain*.

Moreover, expanding our evaluation to a multi-model approach suggests a bit more nuance in what Proust is doing. Figure 41 shows a smoothing of many more models. If there is a flat selection, it likely starts further into the narrative. It's also likely that with this "person-on-the-plain" there are some smaller curves like we've seen in other simpler shapes. Is this shape indicative of the English translation, or can it be surfaced in the original French? Those wishing for a clear answer will be disappointed because comparing translation and original proved harder than expected. In French we now have models like FlauBERT and CamemBERT in addition to a multilingual RoBERTa. Other options include a multilingual NLPtown and a lexicon-based VADER. While we were optimistic, what we found was that the transformer models diverged quite drastically from each other, and a comparison between both English translations and the French resulted in vastly different models, many of which held little resemblance to each other. As a comparatist trained to work in multiple languages, I am sad to report that we don't yet have great models for many languages. Not all models agree and, for this text, the simpler model, VADER, seemed to work best for now.

---

[21] Proust continually revised and edited his work, so disentangling exactly what he had written before the award is somewhat unclear, although many scholars have worked to document the manuscript's evolution.

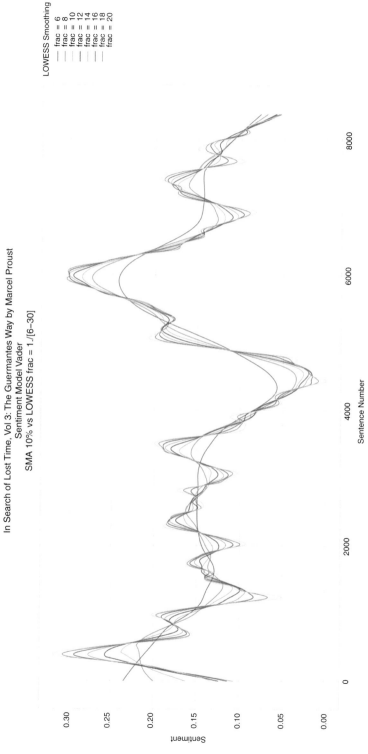

Figure 41 SMA versus LOWESS smoothed sentiment of Proust's *The Guermantes Way*

3.5 Translated Curves

Do different translations of the same text have different sentiment arcs? We first explored this question with our digital humanities fellow, Erin Shaheen, who proposed examining whether Emily Wilson's new landmark translation of Homer's *Odyssey* differed in ways that could be detected by our model. Here is yet another instance in which the answer is more complicated than first glance would suggest. For simplicity, I'll show only the simplest model (Syuzhet) since that is how we began the project. Wilson's translation is shown in Figure 42. Comparing her sentiment arc to other English translations spanning hundreds of years, from George Chapman's 1611 version to Ian Johnston's 2002 version, one is struck by the fact that changes cannot be accounted for chronologically – in other words, as increasingly "modern" versions. In fact, general semantic features like sentiment are surprisingly robust in the face of shifting language and word distributions. When examining the granular fingerprint in gray, you can see that there are two other translations with very similar arcs to Wilson's, Cowper's from 1791 (Figure 43), and Butler's (Figure 44) from 1900. Others diverge, most notably in the second half of the narrative, after the major hole shape. Some graph the second peak lower, so that the hole shape is replaced by a shape that looks entirely different and very like Woolf's *To the Lighthouse*, as can be seen in Figure 45. Fagles (Figure 46) and Johnston (Figure 47) differ by graphing the ending portion near or above neutral, as opposed to in negative territory, mirroring the earlier translation by Alexander Pope (Figure 48). Butcher offers even more positivity for that later section of the narrative, as seen in Figure 49.

Chapman's Homer, seen in Figure 50, is a dark outlier, offering waves that fall almost entirely below neutral and diverging quite significantly from all other transitions we examined. Notice how these differences, most of which are relatively modest changes in intensity, can drastically affect the simplest shape, turning it from a person-in-a-hole shape to descending storyteller curves. The simplest shapes, as we've already seen, can greatly distort minor changes, leading to our first impression that translations differ more drastically than they do. Our first impression confirmed our sense of the crucial, creative role of the translator. A more fine-grained approach that investigates the SMA peaks and valleys – as opposed to a comparison of general DCT shapes – suggests that most translators retain the same general sentiment arc with differences in peak valence and intensity located in the later part of the narrative.

There is widespread agreement between translations for the first peak, which occurs when Odysseus begins the story of his travels. The tale descends into

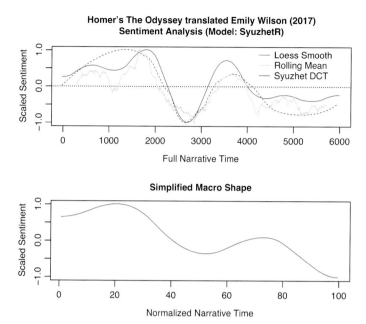

Figure 42 Smoothed sentiment of Homer's *Odyssey* (translated by Wilson, 2018)

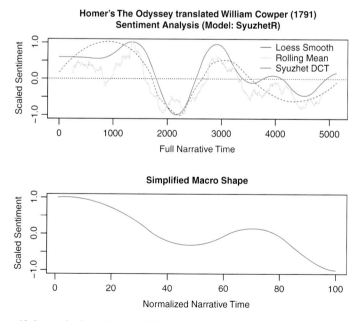

Figure 43 Smoothed sentiment of Homer's *Odyssey* (translated by Cowper, 1791)

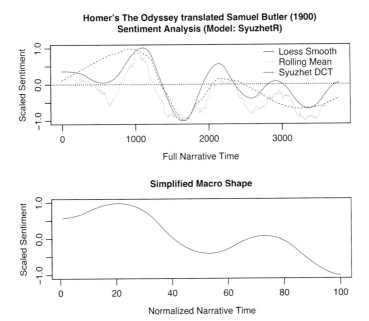

Figure 44 Smoothed sentiment of Homer's *Odyssey* (translated by Butler, 1900)

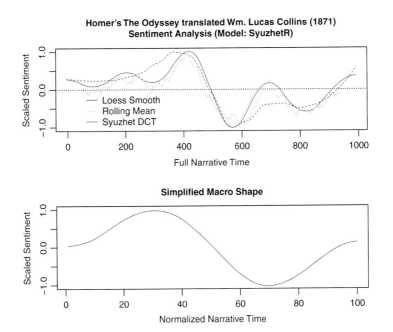

Figure 45 Smoothed sentiment of Homer's *Odyssey* (translated by Collins, 1871)

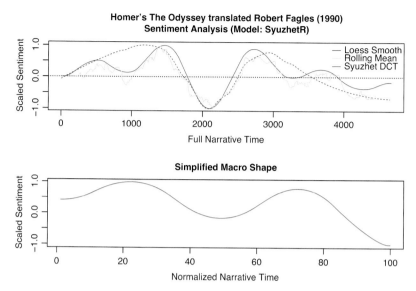

Figure 46 Smoothed sentiment of Homer's *Odyssey* (translated by Fagles, 1996)

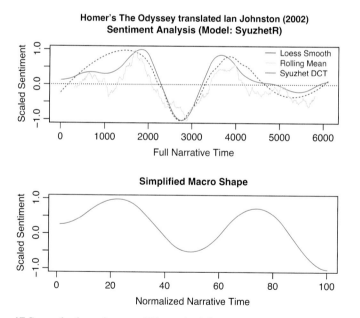

Figure 47 Smoothed sentiment of Homer's *Odyssey* (translated by Johnston, 2002)

some of the most tragic events of the journey and then begins a climb out of the hole as he is able to evade snares more successfully, as, for example, when avoiding the lure of the sirens. The second peak occurs with his arrival back on

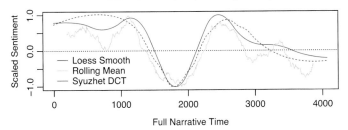

Figure 48 Smoothed sentiment of Homer's *Odyssey*
(translated by Pope, 1726)

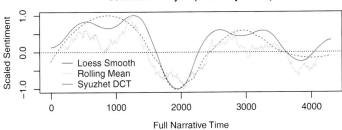

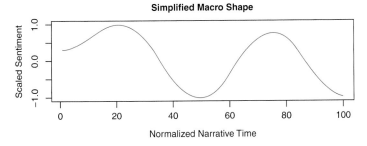

Figure 49 Smoothed sentiment of Homer's *Odyssey*
(translated by Butcher and Lang, 1879)

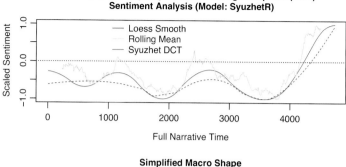

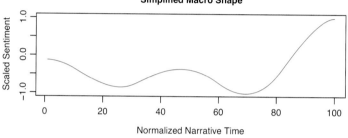

Figure 50 Smoothed sentiment of Homer's *Odyssey*
(translated by Chapman, 1611)

Ithaca, albeit in disguised form. The events back in the castle with Penelope and the rivalry of the suitors occur during the second valley, before the final scenes of reconciliation between husband and wife.

Now for the points of divergence between translations. When Odysseus finds himself finally back on Ithaca, is this peak as high as the first, when he begins his journey home, or does it occur quite a bit lower? Some translations suggest sentiment that equals the first peak. Others temper the emotion of this home-coming so that we lose the "person-in-a-hole" structure. Similarly, the ending is graphed at different emotional valences depending on translation. Do we imagine the final reconciliation as positive? Or does the slaughter of the suitors, as well as Penelope's offer to remarry before she learns of Odysseus's return, darken our sense of the final reconciliation? Emily Wilson's translation stands out for the relatively low valence of the ending, though it is certainly far from alone in this aspect. Butler's translation shares a similar pessimism.

Once again, middle reading offers us a middle ground. Is the task of the translator that of a creator in their own right, such that each translation creates its own unique fingerprint? Not quite. Are there choices in the language of senti-ment that, with subtle changes, can alter the overall arc, emphasizing or obscuring a simple shape? Yes, absolutely.

3.6 Poetic Curves

Questions of translation also appear in another one of our explorations, this one using comparative arcs to surface two different sections of the same text, *Pale Fire*. This novel by Vladimir Nabokov has proven remarkably resistant to critical approaches. The first section is a poem written by the fictional John Shade and the second is an endnote commentary by the fictional faux-scholar Charles Kinbote. One central question is whether the first and second sections are connected. Kinbote is an unreliable narrator and the notes often seem to have very little to do with the poem, instead veering off into stories – made up or having occurred in the realm of the narrative is unclear – about Kinbote's life before exile. Is Kinbote's commentary truly relevant to Shade's poem, or is he parasitically using the poem as a vehicle for his narcissistic reflections? Is Shade's poem a translation into poetry of Kinbote's life story, as Kinbote claims? Or do poem and commentary have little, if any, relation to each other at all?

Both the poem and commentary have fairly strong underlying narrative elements. Still we wondered whether each would show a strong sentiment arc, especially the poem. To our surprise, Syuzhet was able to surface a sentiment arc for the poem. Less surprising was the arc that surfaced in the commentary. Though the endnote-like structure seems inimical to sentiment arc, anyone who's read *Pale Fire* will know that embedded in the notes is a very entertaining tale.

Can sentiment arc give us any additional clues with which to try to understand a notoriously tricky narrative? Some hesitation is warranted in a recommendation to break a novel into multiple sections. More data yield a stronger signal, and here we are opting for less data. Our student Catherine Perloff suggested experimenting this way, and we're glad she did. What is striking when put side by side is how poetry and commentary form almost mirror images of each other. *Almost*, it should be stressed, because for the poem (Figure 51) to mirror the commentary exactly (Figure 52), the first dip would need to be less extreme. There is some slight distortion in the mirroring.

Indeed one might say that the doubling or reflection seen in the sentiment arcs mirrors the novel's title, which invokes Shakespeare. *Pale Fire* is taken from Shakespeare's *Timon of Athens*, and many like to quote only the lines that reference the moon, which steals light from the sun. A common reading of the novel is that Kinbote, the critic, is like the moon, reflecting only a bit of the fire from the poem, the sun. Kinbote's notes are at best a pale reflection of the original. Kinbote, of course, insists that Shade's poem is the reflection since it takes its inspiration from Kinbote's story of being king, which he claims to have told Shade on their walks. And of course Shade's name should make us hesitate to take his poem as the original source of light.

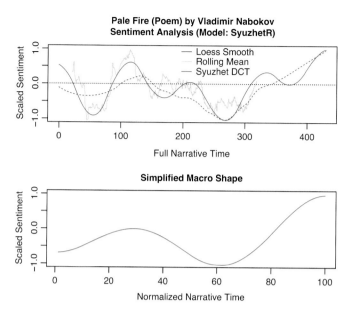

Figure 51 Smoothed sentiment of Nabokov's *Pale Fire* (Poem)

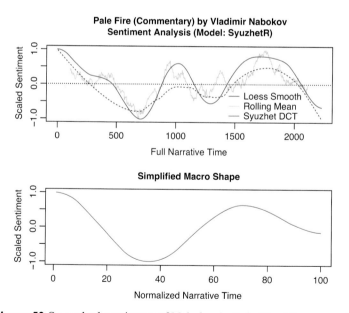

Figure 52 Smoothed sentiment of Nabokov's *Pale Fire* (Commentary)

Perhaps a more granular inspection will offer further insight. In the poem there are two valleys on either side of 300. These valleys surface the moment in the poem when Shade recounts waiting for his daughter to return home. She,

meanwhile, walks into a nearby lake in an apparent suicide. The second valley
recounts the poet's ensuing grief. Other dips occur during the speaker's near-
death experiences. The poem meditates on what lies on the other side of death –
is it a mirror image of this existence? In fact, the poet suggests, we have not gone
far enough in imagining it to be entirely different. Instead we imagine death to
be a pale imitation of this life, only without the emotional sorrows and the
bodily experiences.

Now for the peaks of the poem. One occurs when the narrator professes faith
in love. This profession directly follows a brief encomium to the Vanessa
butterfly, whose metamorphosis from one self to another offers a radical transformation of self unlike the pale imitation some imagine of life after death:

> Four thousand times your pillow has been creased
> By our two heads. Four hundred thousand times
> The tall clock with the hoarse Westminster chimes
> Has marked our common hour. How many more
> Free calendars shall grace the kitchen door?
>
> I love you when you're standing on the lawn
> Peering at something in a tree: "It's gone.
> It was so small. It might come back" (all this
> Voiced in a whisper softer than a kiss).
> I love you when you call me to admire
> A jet's pink trail above the sunset fire.

The second peak surfaces as Shade is about to meet a woman who is reported to
have had the same near-death vision as himself. However, he discovers that the
story contains a typo and where he saw a mountain, she saw a fountain. The poet
concludes with an affirmation that this "rhyming" model for life, in which near
similarity is always accompanied by a slight difference, is a consolation.

In Shade's case an experience that he believed to be identical turned out to be
a mirror experience with a "rhyming" component. Are the two sections of the
novel also almost mirror images but with rhyming variations? A longer excerpt
from Shakespeare's description of pale fire suggests that all identities steal from
another and that no identity is original:

> I'll example you with thievery:
> The sun's a thief, and with his great attraction
> Robs the vast sea; the moon's an arrant thief,
> And her pale fire she snatches from the sun;
> The sea's a thief, whose liquid surge resolves
> The moon into salt tears; the earth's a thief,
> That feeds and breeds by a composture stolen
> From general excrement: each thing's a thief.

Each element steals from and reflects the other in some "pale" way. It is a fitting title, one that suggests that neither Shade nor Kinbote offer us an original. It should make us hesitate to imagine that Kinbote is mad to believe the poem reflects his life in some muted fashion. Sentiment analysis suggests both "stories" surface mirror curves with slight distortions. Are there any thematic resonances in the cruxes that might support this claim?

In the commentary the lowest valley occurs when the king is escaping into exile. Climbing high into the mountains, he sees a butterfly right before he leans over a mountain lake and sees his reflection. At the same time, one of his supporters, dressed as his double to throw off the search party, leans over from high above, causing the king to experience a sense of the uncanny. This moment is his final moment as king since he then dons a disguise and lives on in exile as another self with an altogether different life. The butterfly and the lake mirror the valley in the poem, when the poet's daughter walks into the lake to explore what lies on the other side. But here there is a slight difference: the king metaphorically dies while his new alter ego lives on.

Both Shade and Kinbote experience something akin to "life after death," with Kinbote's new version as a professor far more extreme – and to some unbelievable – like the metamorphosis of a butterfly. Still their valleys differ since Shade recounts the death of his daughter in a lake. Kinbote's metaphorical death is instead symbolized by gazing into a lake and seeing his mirror reflection, multiplied. A later dip occurs when Gradus, his pursuer, looks over a pool and sees the sandals left by Narcissus. This second valley in the commentary section therefore offers a pale reflection of the commentary's first valley. Does looking into a lake show only one's own reflection, or does it reveal a moment when one sees another and imagines a different self?

As you can see, the reflections in the two sections' arcs both mirror and deepen our understanding of thematic elements of the novel. To return to our original question: do Kinbote's notes have anything to do with the poem? It would seem that the relationship is a reflection, which is always an imperfect representation of the original. It is as though each text is a lake for the other. The reflection in the lake is always distorted, different, even as the specter of Narcissus haunts any reflection. In proof of Kinbote's claim that his notes do in fact help further our understanding of the poem, we could say that they repeat the sentiment arc, albeit imperfectly. On the other hand, one could also say that they reverse the sentiment arc as a mirror image, thus flipping the significance entirely. One highlights the tragic descent and the other the gradual ascent out of darkness.

Of course, in Shakespeare's extended metaphor, no element keeps what it steals in its original form, and we can see this too in the way the arcs reflect each other rather than reproduce each other. Perhaps what the sentiment arcs suggest, like the longer quote that surrounds "Pale Fire," is a more complex sense that multiple reflections complicate any single identity. Before one begins to put too much emphasis on the reflection, however, it's important to stress that maybe the uniqueness of each graph is more important than the similarity: the difference between the fountain and the mountain is but one letter and yet the gulf is vast. The thematic resonances in the cruxes suggest a shared pattern. But when one adds models, especially the transformers, the differences multiply and the similarities threaten to disappear. Of the models that I typically use to do a cluster analysis, only RoBERTa, Flair, and Syuzhet surface the peaks one would expect in the poem. When it comes to the commentary, these three comport, as well as SentimentR (Jockers/Rinker). Nabokov's meditation on pale fire and reflections reminds us that while all stories might have similar shapes, the distortions are often what make a particular story enjoyable – even when, or perhaps especially when, the distortions make us question how closely one copies another.

3.7 Life Writing

Nabokov's novel begs yet another question: do life stories have sentiment arcs? *The Narrative of the Life of Frederick Douglass* provides an interesting case study since Douglass explicitly calls his story a narrative. Scholars have even noted the ways in which certain scenes invoke genres like the picaresque or sentimental fiction. Indeed Douglass seems to be well aware of his craft, offering us storyteller curves as shown in Figure 53.

Clustered close reading of peaks using an ensemble model surfaces learning to read as a path to freedom (approx. 440), and arriving at Mr. Freeland's house, whose treatment was "heavenly" in comparison with earlier experiences (1120) and is the first time Douglass creates a strong social network. Reading offers a first step to freedom, which Douglass will then pass on to others. The second scene in which Douglass teaches others to read is also represented as a crux peak, but it is a peak in the larger valley of Chapter X.

A clustered close reading reveals two other peaks, one shared by most models and another that stands out as an unusual outlier in only a few. The shared peak occurs near the beginning of the narrative (approx. 180) during the description of the singing at Great Home Farm. Only after describing this joyful singing does Douglass explain that the joy disguises a longing for freedom communicated in song, a longing that even he, as a young boy, did not understand. Is sentiment analysis wrong to surface this crux, given that a moment of seeming joy is actually representative of its opposite? Perhaps, though the singing, it

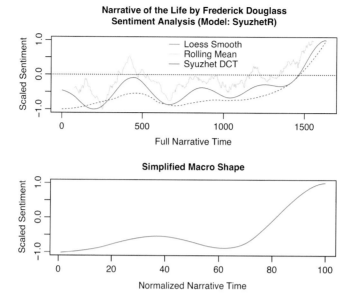

Figure 53 Smoothed sentiment of Frederick Douglass's *Narrative of the Life of Frederick Douglass: An American Slave*

might be argued, represents one of the few moments of freedom of expression (albeit coded), a freedom that prefigures Douglass's own expression in the narrative we read.

The second outlier crux surfaces midway through the narrative. Hugging Face locates a peak when describing the deceitful religiosity of Mr. Covey. Here the false piety is described in terms that confuse this particular model, just as many might mistake Mr. Covey's surface piety for reality. This is what Jon Chun and I term a *surface crux*, a surface emotion that mimics the phenomenon Douglass outlines and that highlights the need to interpret what lies beneath. One more divergence occurs soon thereafter in Douglass's fight with Mr. Covey. This is represented as a small sentiment peak by one model (RoBERTa, 972). Here there seems to be more reason to think that this turning point, while infused with violence, is nonetheless an important moment of inflection when, as Douglass writes, "the slave becomes a man." For this reason it's interesting that RoBERTa is able to locate it as a sentiment peak, however attenuated.

Valleys in the narrative surface an interesting structural aspect. They often focus on others' stories. Here we see the skillful way in which Douglass weaves "the many" into his narrative, making his life story one that represents more than just his own experience. One such valley portrays the execution of Demby by the cruel Mr. Gore (approx. 280). Another recounts the beating of his Aunt Hester. Only later do we see Douglass's own experiences recounted during emotional valleys, when he describes extreme hunger (approx. 689), his contemplation of suicide, (893), and his beating while working in the shipyard (1359).

This phenomenon, in which cruxes extend to others' experiences, is not quite the same as the distributed heroine we saw in *To the Lighthouse*. In Douglass's case the events are recounted from his perspective. He thus serves as both witness and emotional participant since the cruxes unite both his story and that of others. His sentiment arc emphasizes that witnessing these events is inevitably to be a participant in such, with a united sentiment. White slaveholders are implicated as well since Douglass creates a sentiment arc that surfaces the moral degradation that is a consequence of slaveholding.

What is the sense of the ending? Some graphs note the downward turn, and this seems in keeping with the sense of loss that accompanies freedom. Douglass's own freedom is tempered by the acute sense of a loss of community as he leaves many behind in misery. In terms of a more general shape, however, models surface different degrees of intensification, and these differences suggest divergent, simpler shapes of the narrative. Those that represent lower positive emotional valence create more of a person-in-the-hole story. Those models that surface higher peaks resemble more of the storyteller curves. Scholars similarly disagree on the simpler shape of the story. Some have suggested the narrative has elements of the episodic picaresque, which would substantiate models that surface storyteller curves. Others have suggested a rags-to-riches upward rise more consonant with the muted peaks and gradual rise of the person-in-the-hole.

Yet others have suggested that Douglass's story is a conversion narrative. To explore this possibility further, I turn now to one of the first examples of life writing that is also a conversion story: Augustine's *Confessions*. Modeling *Confessions* highlights a number of challenges. First, we still don't have good tools for surfacing sentiment in Latin, though at least one is in development (Sprugnoli, 2021). Also a confounding factor may be the extensive prayers embedded in the narrative, which could alter the sentiment arc but could also be considered part of Augustine's own distributed hero. Finally, the narrative turns from life writing to theological and philosophical concerns in the final books, so only the first nine books truly represent life writing.

Our first experiments were with a simple model and we limited our investigation to the first nine books in translation seen in Figure 54. What happens when we move to a multi-model analysis and include the later chapters that are more theo-philosophical in nature? Most models surface

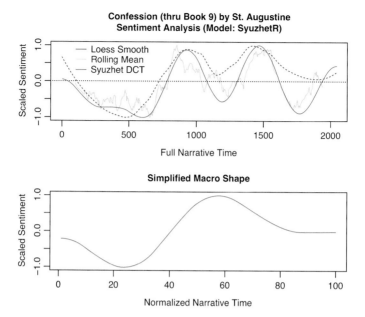

Figure 54 Smoothed sentiment of St. Augustine's *Confessions* (through Book IX)

a gradually rising series of storyteller curves that continue even into the later chapters. In fact, we find that the upward trajectory continues with the exception of a very strong dip in Book XI.

Low points are often communal in some form, whether they depict falling in among the wrong crowd (approx. 480) or the moment when Alypius joins Augustine in a devotion to Manichaeism. As in Douglass, a moment of reading occurs in the first peak, when Augustine reads the Neoplatonists (peak 1347) but later in a valley, before conversion, when Augustine reads the Bible in the garden (valley, 1679). The similarity in sentiment arcs, a similarity that extends even to thematic concerns surrounding reading, does indeed suggest that Douglass's narrative evinces elements of a conversion story. Augustine's *Confessions* is notable for creating a pattern for a tradition of narrative life writing that continues in more modern instances.

3.8 How Stories Feel

At the most basic level, sentiment analysis can't tell us what we really wish to know: how stories feel to us. Rather, it tells us how stories themselves "feel" – how stories can embody a language of sentiment independent of character or readerly experience. Every reader is different, and more research into sentiment arcs may help us begin to explore these differences. It's also important to understand that different cultural groups may feel stories differently, both because the language resonates differently and because the events hold different contextual meaning. This exploration of the difference in the ways stories feel to different individuals and groups is one that sentiment analysis may help us advance to the extent that it helps us begin a dialogue about these different ways of feeling particular arcs and crux points.

Others are exploring ways that characters feel in stories, as Kim and Klinger are doing. Jhavar and Mirza (2018) are mapping emotions of relationships in stories. All of this work builds on earlier work that explores the role of emotion in reading (Mar et al., 2011) and even suggests that stories may provide a prime vehicle for understanding human emotion (Hogan, 2010). But sentiment analysis, as I've argued, is agnostic about how stories feel to us. Some experiments in the science of storytelling seem to confirm that reactions to stories may fall into fairly simple sentiment responses. Paul J. Zak, for example, has explored the secretion of neurochemicals like cortisol and oxytocin that give rise to feelings of distress or empathy/connection.

At the same time, these approaches offer more avenues for detailed investigation of cultural differences. When we ask how a story feels to us, we always have to ask who, after all, is "us"? When reading a narrative written by a member of a culture with which I am less familiar, how do I know that I'm interpreting the scene in a way that would make sense to those from the culture? And what about intra-cultural differences? This is one reason we advocate building an annotated corpus in which we can crowdsource interpretative cruxes. Could sentiment analysis actually help us in our endeavors to be readers who are more sensitive to cultural differences? How stories feel to us is no doubt quite different depending on who we mean by "us."

Examples like these highlight the extent to which we need not just a human-in-the-loop but many humans-in-the-loop. It also points to the need for a more diverse corpus, and this poses some challenges since the texts easily available on Project Gutenberg don't offer us the diversity we seek. To go beyond these readily available narratives, one has to have access to digitization tools like we do, and this raises further questions of access. My hope is that those with access to these tools will make the digitized arcs available to many to analyze, ideally in a low-code environment. This is because there are still many pressing research questions waiting to be answered, and the more we compare what we find, the more we can discover about how stories feel.

Appendix

Sentiment Arcs

Rowling, *Harry Potter and the Deathly Hallows*
Shakespeare, *Romeo and Juliet*
Joyce, *Portrait of the Artist As a Young Man*
Cinderella
Woolf, *To the Lighthouse*
Dickens, *Great Expectations*
Woolf, *Orlando*
    Mrs. Dalloway
    The Waves
James, *Portrait of a Lady*
Eliot, *Middlemarch*
Defoe, *The Life and Adventures of Robinson Crusoe*
Homer, *Odyssey*
Conrad, *Heart of Darkness*
Morrison, *Beloved*
McEwan, *Machines Like Me*
Proust, *Swann's Way*
    In the Shadow of Young Girls in Flower
    The Guermantes Way
    Sodom and Gomorrah
    Le Côté de Guermantes
Homer, *Odyssey* (nine translations)
Nabokov, *Pale Fire*
Douglass, *Narrative of the Life of Frederick Douglass*
Augustine, *Confessions*

References

Achebe, Chinua. "An Image of Africa: Racism in Conrad's *Heart of Darkness*." *Massachusetts Review*, vol. 57, no. 1, 2016, pp. 14–27.

Archer, Jodie, and Jockers, Matthew. *The Bestseller Code*. St. Martin's Press, 2016.

Aristotle. *Poetics*. Trans. Anthony Kenny. Oxford University Press, 2013.

Augustine. *The Confessions of Saint Augustine*. Project Gutenberg. Last updated May 2013. www.gutenberg.org/files/3296/3296-h/3296-h.htm

Barid, Mimun, Hossain, Shahadat, Rahman, Mahmudur, and Hasan, Manzurul. "Sentiment Analysis Applying the Big 5 and Polarity on the ICC's Top ODI All- Rounders Based on Twitter." In *2021 24th International Conference on Computer and Information Technology (ICCIT)*, 2021, pp. 1–5.

Blatt, Ben. *Nabokov's Favorite Word Is Mauve*. Simon and Schuster, 2017.

Booker, Christopher. *The Seven Basic Plots: Why We Tell Stories*. Bloomsbury Continuum, 2019.

Books, List of best-selling. https://en.wikipedia.org/wiki/List_of_best-selling_books

Boyd, Ryan, Blackburn, Kate, and Pennebaker, James. "The Narrative Arc: Revealing Core Structures through Text Analysis." *Science Advances*, vol. 6, no. 32, August 2020.

Bugg, John. "How Radical Was Joseph Johnson and Why Does Radicalism Matter?" *Studies in Romanticism*, vol. 57, no. 2, 2018, pp. 173–195.

Campbell, Joseph. *The Hero with a Thousand Faces*. New World Library, 2008.

Cavendar, Kurt, Graham, Jamey, Fox, Robert, Flynn, Richard, and Cavender, Kenyon. "Body Language: Toward an Affective Formalism of *Ulysses*." In *Reading Modernism with Machines*. Ed. Ross, Shawna and O'Sullivan, James. Palgrave, 2016, pp. 223–241.

Chun, Jon. "SentimentArcs: A Novel Method for Self-Supervised Sentiment Analysis of Time Series Shows SOTA Transformers Can Struggle Finding Narrative Arcs." arXiv. arXiv/abs 2110.09454 (2021)

Chun, Jon, and Elkins, Katherine. "What the Rise of AI Means for Narrative Studies." *Narrative*, vol. 30, no. 1, January 2022, pp. 104–113.

Conrad, Joseph. *Heart of Darkness*. Project Gutenberg. Last updated January 2021. www.gutenberg.org/files/219/219-h/219-h.htm

Crawford, Kate. *The Atlas of AI*. Yale University Press, 2021.

Culler, Jonathan. "Story and Discourse in the Analysis of Narrative." Chapter 8 in *The Pursuit of Signs*. Cornell University Press, 2002, pp. 169–187.

Da, Nan Z. "The Computational Case against Computational Literary Studies." *Critical Inquiry*, vol. 45, no. 3, 2019, pp. 601–639.

Dashtipour, Kia, Poria, Soujanya, Hussain, Amir, et al. "Multilingual Sentiment Analysis: State of the Art: State of the Art and Independent Comparison of Techniques." *Cognitive Computation* 8 (2016), pp. 757–777.

Defoe, Daniel. *The Life and Adventures of Robinson Crusoe*. Project Gutenberg. Last updated January 2021. www.gutenberg.org/files/521/521-h/521-h.htm

Dickens, Charles. *Great Expectations*. Project Gutenberg. Last updated April 2020. www.gutenberg.org/files/1400/1400-h/1400-h.htm

Douglass, Frederick. *Narrative of the Life of Frederick Douglass*. Project Gutenberg. Last updated February 2021. www.gutenberg.org/files/23/23-h/23-h.htm

EAB. "The 15 most-assigned books at the top 30 U.S. colleges." June 11, 2018. https://eab.com/insights/daily-briefing/workplace/the-15-most-assigned-books-at-the-top-30-u-s-colleges

Eliot, George. *Middlemarch*. Project Gutenberg. Last updated January 2021. www.gutenberg.org/files/145/145-0.txt

Elkins, Katherine, and Chun, Jon. "Can GPT-3 Pass a Writer's Turing Test?" *Journal of Cultural Analytics*, vol. 5:2, September 14, 2020.

"Can Sentiment Analysis Reveal Structure in a Plotless Novel?" arXiv. arXiv/abs1910.01441 (2019)

"Woolf's Plotless Novels and Reparative Narratives." *Modernist Studies Association*, 2019. www.academia.edu/44702769/Woolfs_Plotless_Novels_and_Reparative_Narratives_Sentiment_Analysis_and_the_Modernist_Novel

Elvis. "Examining Gender and Race Bias in Sentiment Analysis." *Medium*, August 2, 2018. https://medium.com/dair-ai/examining-gender-and-race-bias-in-sentiment-analysis-systems-b04b269a653

Flowingdata.com. "Bible Sentiment Analysis." October 17, 2011. https://flowingdata.com/2011/10/17/bible-sentiment-analysis

Freytag, Gustav. *Technique of the Drama*. University Press of the Pacific, 2004.

Frye, Northrop. *The Great Code: The Bible and Literature*. Mariner Books, 2002.

Gao, Jianbo, Jockers, Matthew, Laudun, John, and Tangherlini, Timothy. "A Multiscale Theory for the Dynamical Evolution of Sentiment in Novels." In *2016 International Conference on Behavioral, Economic and Socio-cultural Computing (BESC)*, 2016, pp. 1–4.

Harmon, Dan. "Dan Harmon's Story Circle." June 15, 2020. www.youtube.com /watch?v=RG4WcRAgm7Y

"The Hedonometer." Hedonometer, hedonometer.org/books/v1/?lens=[3,7].

Hogan, Patrick. "Fictions and Feelings: On the Place of Literature in the Study of Emotion." *Emotion Review*, vol. 2, 2010, pp. 184–195.

Homer. *The* Odyssey. Trans. Samuel Butcher and Andrew Lang. New York, 1879. http://johnstoniatexts.x10host.com/homer/butcherlangodyssey.htm

Homer. *The Odyssey*. Trans. Samuel Butler. A.C. Fifield,1900. https://en .wikisource.org/wiki/The_Odyssey_(Butler)

Homer. *The Odyssey*. Trans. Lucas Collins. Blackwood, 1871.

Homer. *Odyssey*. Trans. William Cowper. J. Johnson, 1790. https://en.wikisource .org/wiki/The_Iliad_and_Odyssey_of_Homer_(Cowper)/Volume_2

Homer. *The* Odyssey. Trans. Robert Fagles. Penguin, 1996.

Homer. *The Odyssey*. Trans. Ian Johnston. Richer Resources, 2002.

Homer. *The Odyssey*. Trans. Alexander Pope. Tinsley and Widger, 1726. Last updated July 20201. www.gutenberg.org/files/3160/3160-h/3160-h.htm

Homer. *The* Odyssey. Trans. Emily Wilson. W.W. Norton & Company, 2018.

Hu, Qiyue, Liu, Bin, Thomsen, Mads, Gao, Jianbo, and Nielbo, Kristoffer. "Dynamic Evolution of Sentiments in *Never Let Me Go*: Insights from Quantitative Analysis and Implications." In *2019 6th International Conference on Behavioral, Economic and Socio-cultural Computing (BESC)*, 2019, pp. 1–6.

James, Henry. *Portrait of a Lady*. 2 vols. Project Gutenberg. www.gutenberg.org /ebooks/2833, www.gutenberg.org/files/2834/2834-h/2834-h.htm

Jhavar, Harshita, and Mirza, Paramita. "EMOFIEL: Mapping Emotions of Relationships in a Story." In *Companion Proceedings of the Web Conference 2018*.

Jockers, Matthew. *Macroanalysis*. University of Illinois Press, 2013.

"Revealing Sentiment and Plot Arcs with the Syuzhet Package: Matthew L. Jockers." *Matthew Jockers*. February 2, 2015. www.matthewjockers.net /2015/02/02/syuzhet

"That Sentimental Feeling: Matthew L. Jockers." *Matthew Jockers*. December 20, 2015. www.matthewjockers.net/2015/12/20/that-sentimental-feeling

Jones, Charles. "*Easily* in the Middle." Proceedings of the Western Conference on Linguistics, vol. 19, 2008.

Jung, Carl Gustav. *The Archetypes and the Collective Unconscious*. Routledge, 1991.

Kaushal, Prajwal, Bharadwaj, Nithin, Pranav, MS, Koushik, S, and Koundinya, Anjan. "Myers-Briggs Personality Prediction and Sentiment Analysis of Twitter using Machine Learning Classifiers and BERT." *International Journal of Information Technology and Computer Science*, vol. 6, 2021, pp. 48–60.

Kermode, Frank. *The Sense of an Ending*. Oxford University Press, 1967.

Kim, Evgeny and Klinger, Roman. "An Analysis of Emotion Communication Channels in Fan Fiction: Towards Emotional Storytelling." arXiv. arXiv/abs1906.02402 (2019)

"A Survey on Sentiment and Emotion Analysis for Computational Literary Studies." arXiv. arXiv/abs1808.03137 (2018)

Kim, Evgeny, Padó, Sebastian, and Klinger, Roman. "Investigating the Relationship between Literary Genres and Emotional Plot Development."*ACL Anthology,* August 2017. https://aclanthology.org/W17-2203

Kiritchenko, Svetlana, and Mohammad, Saif. "Examining Gender and Race Bias in Two Hundred Sentiment Analysis Systems." arXiv. arXiv/abs1805.04508 (2018)

Kramer, David. "*Adam Bede* and the Development of Early Modernism." *George Eliot – George Henry Lewes Studies*, no. 36/37, September 1999, pp. 59–69.

LaFrance, Adrienne. "The Six Main Stories, As Identified by a Computer." *The Atlantic*, November 1, 2018. www.theatlantic.com/technology/archive/2016/07/the-six-main-arcs-in-storytelling-identified-by-a-computer/490733

Lei, Lei, and Liu, Dilin. *Conducting Sentiment Analysis*. Cambridge University Press, 2021.

Levi-Strauss, Claude. *Myth and Meaning*. Schocken, 1995.

Mika, Graziotin, Daniel, and Kuutila, Miika. "The Evolution of Sentiment Analysis: A Review of Research Topics, Venues, and Top Cited Papers." arXiv. arXiv/abs1612.01556 (2018)

Mar, Raymond, Oatley, Keith, Djikic, Maja, and Mullin, Justin. "Emotion and Narrative Fiction: Interactive Influences before, during, and after Reading. *Cognition and Emotion*, vol. 25, 2011, pp. 818–833.

McEwan, Ian. *Machines Like Me*. Doubleday, 2019.

Mohammad, Saif, Bravo-Marquez, Felipe, Salameh, Mohammad, and Kiritchenko, Svetlana. "SemEval-2018 Task 1: Affect in Tweets." *ACL Anthology*, June 2018. https://aclanthology.org/S18-1001/

Morin, Olivier, and Acerbi, Alberto. "Birth of the Cool: A Two-Centuries Decline in Emotional Expression in Anglophone Fiction." *Cognition and Emotion*, vol. 31, 2017, pp. 1663–1675.

Mulholland, James. *Before the Raj: Writing Early Anglophone India*. Johns Hopkins University Press, 2021.

Piper, Andrew. *Can We Be Wrong?* Cambridge University Press, 2020.

Enumerations. University of Chicago Press, 2018.

Propp, Vladimir. *Morphology of a Folktale*. Trans. Laurence Scott. Martino, 2015.

Proust, Marcel. *A la recherche du temps perdu*. Project Gutenberg, 2001–2020. www.gutenberg.org/ebooks/author/987

In Search of Lost Time. General Editor, Prendergast, Christopher. Penguin, 2002.

Remembrance of Things Past. Project Gutenberg Australia. https://gutenberg .net.au/plusfifty-n-z.html#proust

Reagan, Andrew J., et al. "The Emotional Arcs of Stories Are Dominated by Six Basic Shapes." *EPJ Data Science*, vol. 5, no. 1, 2016. https://epjda tascience.springeropen.com/articles/10.1140/epjds/s13688-016-0093-1

Rinker, Tyler. Sentimentr. https://github.com/trinker/sentimentr

Rosenthal, Caitlin. "Seeking a Quantitative Middle Ground: Reflections on Methods and Opportunities in Economic History." *Journal of the Early Republic*, vol. 36, no. 4, Winter 2016, pp. 659–680.

Schmidt, Ben. "Plot Arceology 2016: Emotion and Tension." *Sapping Attention*, July 18, 2016. http://sappingattention.blogspot.com/2016/07/ plot-arceology-emotion-and-tension.html

Senderle, Jonathan. "A Plot of Brownian Noise." https://senderle.github.io/svd-noise

Sodha, Sean. "Using Watson NLU to Help Address Bias in AI Sentiment Analysis." *IBM.com* Blog, February 12, 2021. www.ibm.com/blogs/wat son/2021/02/watson-nlu-bias-ai-sentiment-analysis

Sprugnoli, Rachele. "Sentiment Analysis for Latin: A Journey from Seneca to Thomas Aquinas." 2021. www.youtube.com/watch?v=SDBL0VRj-8c

Starwars.com. "Mythic Discovery within the Inner Reaches of Outer Space: Joseph Campbell Meets George Lucas." October 22, 2015. www .starwars.com/news/mythic-discovery-within-the-inner-reaches-of-outer-space-joseph-campbell-meets-george-lucas-part-i

Swafford, Annie. "Problems with the Syuzhet Package." March 2, 2015. https:// annieswafford.wordpress.com/2015/03/02/syuzhet

Swanson, Ana. "Researchers Have Quantified What Makes Us Love Harry Potter." *Washington Post*, November 25, 2016. www.washingtonpost.com /news/wonk/wp/2016/11/25/the-six-stories-people-love-most

Taboada, Maite, Gillies, Mary Ann, and McFetridge, Paul. *Sentiment Classification Techniques for Tracking Literary Reputation*. LREC

Workshop, Simon Fraser University, 2006. www.sfu.ca/~mtaboada/docs/research/Taboada_et_al_LREC_Workshop.pdf

Tanveer, M. Iftekhar, Samrose, Samiha, Baten, Raiyan Abdul, and Hoque, M. Ehsan. "Awe the Audience: How the Narrative Trajectories Affect Audience Perception in Public Speaking." *Proceedings of the 2018 CHI Conference on Human Factors in Computing Systems*, April 2018, Paper No. 24, pp. 1–12. https://dl.acm.org/doi/10.1145/3173574.3173598

Tolstoy, Leo. *What Is Art?* Trans. Richard Pevear. Penguin, 1996.

Underwood, Ted. "Free Research Question about Plot." *The Stone and the Shell.* April 2, 2015. tedunderwood.com/2015/04/01/free-research-question-about-plot. Vermont Story Lab.

Vonnegut, Kurt. *Palm Sunday.* Random House, 2010.

Shape of Stories. November 2016. Kurt Vonnegut Lecture. www.youtube.com/watch?v=4_RUgnC1lm8

Woloch, Alex. *The One versus the Many.* Princeton University Press, 2003.

Woolf, Virginia. *Mrs. Dalloway.* Projet Gutenberg Australia. https://gutenberg.net.au/ebooks02/0200991h.html. Most recent update 2002.

Orlando. Project Gutenberg Australia. Most recent update July 2015. http://gutenberg.net.au/ebooks02/0200331.txt

To the Lighthouse. Project Gutenberg Australia. Most Recent Update September 2008. http://gutenberg.net.au/ebooks01/0100101.txt

The Waves. Project Gutenberg Australia. https://gutenberg.net.au/ebooks02/0201091h.html. Most Recent Update 2002.

Yeruva, Vijaya Kumari, Chandreshekar, Mayanka, Leee, Yugyung, Rydberg-Cox, Jeff, Blanton, Virginia, and Oyler, Nathan. "Interpretation of Sentiment Analysis with Human-in-the-Loop." *2020 IEEE International Conference on Big Data (Big Data)*, 2020, pp. 3099–3108.

Zak, Paul J. "Why Inspiring Stories Make Us React: The Neuroscience of Storytelling." *Cerebrum*: The Dana Forum on Brain Science, published online February 2, 2015. www.ncbi.nlm.nih.gov/pmc/articles/PMC4445577

Cambridge Elements ☰

Digital Literary Studies

Katherine Bode

Australian National University

Katherine Bode is Professor of Literary and Textual Studies at the Australian National University. Her research explores the critical potential and limitations of computational approaches to literature, in publications including *A World of Fiction: Digital Collections and the Future of Literary History* (2018), *Advancing Digital Humanities: Research, Methods, Theories* (2014), *Reading by Numbers: Recalibrating the Literary Field* (2012) and *Resourceful Reading: The New Empiricism, eResearch and Australian Literary Culture* (2009).

Adam Hammond

University of Toronto

Adam Hammond is Assistant Professor of English at the University of Toronto. He is author of *Literature in the Digital Age* (Cambridge 2016) and co-author of *Modernism: Keywords* (2014). He works on modernism, digital narrative and computational approaches to literary style. He is editor of the forthcoming *Cambridge Companion to Literature in the Digital Age* and *Cambridge Critical Concepts: Literature and Technology*.

Gabriel Hankins

Clemson University

Gabriel Hankins is Associate Professor of English at Clemson University. His first book is *Interwar Modernism and the Liberal World Order* (Cambridge 2019). He writes on modernism, digital humanities and color. He is technical manager for the Twentieth Century Literary Letters Project and co-editor on *The Digital Futures of Graduate Study in the Humanities* (in progress).

About the Series

Our series provides short exemplary texts that address a pressing research question of clear scholarly interest within a defined area of literary studies, clearly articulate the method used to address the question, and demonstrate the literary insights achieved.

Cambridge Elements ☰

Digital Literary Studies

Printed in the United States
by Baker & Taylor Publisher Services